One Kid at a Time

ONE KID
AT A TIME

**A SINGLE DAD, A BOY IN FOSTER CARE
AND AN ADOPTION**

JAKE DEKKER

NiceTiger

Cover art by Claire Donner and Jake Dekker

Copyright © 2012 by Jake Dekker

NiceTiger
5190 Neil Road, Suite 430
Reno NV 89502
publisher@nicetiger.com
www.nicetiger.com

"*Sing it Loud*" by Joseph Pisapia
© 2011 Campfire Sky Music

"*After Annunciation*" is from
"*The Irrational Season*" by Madeleine L'Engle
© 1977 Crosswicks, Ltd.

"*Hallelujah*" by Leonard Cohen.
© 1985 Sony/ATV Songs, LLC.

ISBN: 978-1-937777-01-2

Library of Congress Cataloging-in-Publication Data available.

To two fine teachers

Linda Anderson
&
Tim Shepherd

Contents

1. Danny   1

2. Jake   8

3. The Birth Dad   18

4. 'Hallelujah'   25

5. The CASA   30

6. Watch and Learn   37

7. First Visit   48

8. First Overnight   54

9. Fourth of July   65

10. Moving In   75

11. Welcome Home Danny   86

12. Week One   98

13. Boo!   105

14. New School   114

15. Parents and Birth Family   123

16. Sisters   132

17. Slap!   137

18. Medication   144
19. Negotiations   155
20. First Christmas   161
21. Adoption Support   169
22. Good News   177
23. Adoption Eve   186
24. Adoption Day   194
25. A New Life   207
26. Eighteen Months Later   213
27. Three Years Later   220

Improving the System   230
The Adoption Process   239

Notes   249
Bibliography   253
Resources   254
Acknowledgments   256
About the Author   258
To the Reader   259

Author's Note

Although this story is based on true facts, I have recreated events, places and conversations from emails, public court records, interviews and my memory of events. Any errors made are my own. In order to maintain the anonymity of actual persons, I have changed most names. To protect my son's privacy, I have written this book under a pseudonym. I have also changed some identifying characteristics and details such as physical properties, occupations and locations. In a few cases, I have changed the gender of an individual. All the details about my son's background were taken from open court records, interviews, emails, letters and other direct sources. All of them, to the best of my knowledge and research, are true. No confidential files given to me by the State of Washington as part of the adoption disclosure were the sole source for any part of this story. My sources for statistics and facts about foster care and outcomes for foster children are attributed by endnotes with sources cited in the *Notes* section at the end of this book.

This is the irrational season
when love blooms bright and wild.
Had Mary been filled with reason
there'd have been no room for the child.
MADELEINE L'ENGLE

Sing it loud, sing it, sing it, sing it loud
So you can remember who you are
K.D. LANG

Ye are the light of the world
JESUS OF NAZARETH

Chapter One

Danny

My son Danny was born January 1998 in Tacoma, Washington; I didn't meet him until he was ten. Two months before he was born, social workers found his 22-year-old birthmother, Wendy, living in an abandoned shipping container. Because she was pregnant, they gave her housing, medical care and food.

Her developmental delays had prevented her from raising her twin daughters, Ashley and Emily, whom she had abandoned at her mother's when they were four.

Wendy didn't have many options. The twins' father wanted nothing to do with his daughters, and Danny's father was uncertain. Wendy never knew her own father; she was the product of rape.

After Danny was born, Wendy moved into housing for low-income mothers. Social workers contacted her regularly, but caring for a baby proved too much. When Danny was nine months old, she abandoned him at her mother's too.

Danny shared the house with Grandma Carol, her 39-year-old alcoholic boyfriend Eddie, their two children, ten-year-old Henry and eight-year-old Annie, and Danny's twin half-sisters who by then were five-years-old. Grandma Carol's 17-year-old son Steven, a known child molester, often stayed in her home.

They all lived in a four-bedroom, one-bath home that was infested with cockroaches and littered with dirty laundry and unwashed dishes. Chunks of ceiling plaster were missing in the dining room, several windows were broken, and the bathroom sink had no running water. The backyard was filled with old vehicles, abandoned appliances, broken bottles and a rusted swing set.

Danny's birthfather, Stan, learned that Danny was his son after taking a paternity test while serving a long prison sentence. When Danny was two, his parents were married. Wendy occasionally visited her mother's house and brought Danny gifts, but she ignored her twin daughters.

When Danny was three, he was taken to the dentist. He had six cavities. Fourteen months later he had 11 more. A social worker noticed black spots on Danny's gums and insisted that Grandma Carol take better care of his teeth.

When Danny was four, his parents divorced and Wendy gave up her legal rights as Danny's mother to Stan. Stan wanted to see Danny regularly, but Grandma Carol didn't like bringing him to visit Stan in prison.

A custody battle ensued between Grandma Carol and Stan's mother, Grandma Doreen. When Danny was five, a judge ordered that he live with Grandma Doreen for three months. After she picked him up, Grandma Carol called the police and reported that Danny had been kidnapped. No charges were filed, as Grandma Doreen had permission to take him. Because of the hostility between them, neither grandmother allowed Danny to talk to the other.

A private social worker was hired to recommend which family Danny should live with. The social worker was appalled by Grandma Carol's house. She was concerned about Grandma Carol and Eddie's inability to hold jobs, Eddie's alcoholism and accusations that Eddie had sexually abused Danny's mother and his own daughter.

Grandma Doreen's house was neat (though it smelled strongly of cat urine) and looked like a better home. Grandma Doreen told the social worker she had worked many years for the state department of disabilities as an aide for handicapped children and that she had never been involved with the child-welfare system. The social worker soon discovered that Grandma Doreen lied; she had 14 referrals for child abuse.

Grandma Doreen and her 24-year-old daughter beat and bruised Danny regularly. Following a particularly brutal incident, his teacher contacted the police when Danny didn't show up at school. Danny was taken into protective custody, and Grandma Doreen was arrested. Quarter-size chunks of hair were missing from his scalp, his face was scratched, several teeth were missing and his chest, back, legs, arms and groin were severely bruised. The doctor who examined Danny told police there were so many bruises she couldn't count them.

The social worker determined that neither home was safe. She sent a 21-page report to the state. Despite her warnings, the state returned Danny to Grandma Carol under the conditions that she fumigate the roaches, clean up the trash in her house and yard, get water running in the bathroom, take parenting classes and keep her registered sex offender son away from Danny.

Two years later, Danny and his sisters were placed in foster care because Grandma Carol kept allowing her sex offender son to be with them. Danny was separated from his sisters. Despite requirements that siblings in foster care have monthly visits, he had little communication with them for the next three years.

In one of his first foster homes, Danny kissed a six-year-old girl on the cheek. When asked why, he replied, "She's like my sister, and I always kiss them goodnight." The state labeled Danny "potentially sexually aggressive," and he wasn't allowed to be unsupervised with children.

Danny seemed hyperactive, so the state requested psychotropic medication to slow him down. The more pills he took, the wilder he became. He was quickly kicked out of his first two foster homes. Danny was angry at school and cried when he was frustrated. He developed a reputation as a difficult kid.

In Washington State, foster children are assigned one of four levels. The level is based on the child's behavior.

The easiest children are assigned a level one, the most difficult a level four. The level determines the monthly payment a foster parent receives. For example, in 2007 caring for a level-one child Danny's age paid $475 a month, and caring for a level-four child paid $1,250 a month.[1]

Danny was diagnosed with attention deficit hyperactivity disorder (ADHD), obsessive-compulsive disorder (OCD), reactive attachment disorder (RAD), post-traumatic stress disorder (PTSD), oppositional defiant disorder (ODD) and possible fetal alcohol spectrum disorder (FASD). Within months of entering foster care, Danny was transformed into a heavily medicated, level-four foster child. He was difficult to control, impulsive and angry.

Because of Danny's labels and behaviors, his social worker struggled to find a foster home. She put him in a home intended for stays of fewer than 30 days. He lived there almost two years. He was fed cups of noodles and frozen cheese pizzas and was usually confined to his bedroom.

Danny's ADHD stimulant medication suppressed his appetite for 12 hours, so he was hungry every night when it wore off. His foster mom wouldn't feed him outside of meal times, so he stole food and hid it in his room. The state's psychiatrist decided to treat Danny's food hoarding by adding Prozac to his other medications. No one realized they could solve the food hoarding concern by simply feeding Danny dinner after his appetite returned.

Whenever he left his room, an alarm alerted his foster mom. She was reprimanded by the state for locking Danny in his room like a cell. He was rarely allowed outside or taken on walks (his foster mom was obese and had mobility issues), and he had little contact with his sisters.

During Danny's first Christmas with his foster mom, she kept him confined in his room while her grandchildren opened gifts and ate their dinner. She told him they didn't want him spoiling their holiday.

He regularly peed in the corner of his bedroom because he didn't want to be yelled at for going to the bathroom at night. Though he was eight years old, he was forced to wear diapers every night so he couldn't wet the bed. His grades and behavior at school deteriorated.

In fourth grade, he was expelled from the school bus for choking and kicking a kindergartener. He was suspended nine times for violence, foul language, stealing food and disrupting class. The school recommended placing him in a special classroom with other emotionally and behaviorally disturbed children, but his teacher asked that Danny remain with her. She argued that placing him with other troubled kids would magnify his problems and that his behaviors were caused by trauma, abandonment and neglect.

She created a special area in her classroom known as Danny's Corner. Danny sat alone, surrounded by three-foot-high walls, with a chance to learn but less opportunity to disrupt the class.

After almost two hellish years in his "temporary" home, Danny escaped by vandalizing his foster mother's new Cadillac. His social worker struggled to find him a new place to live.

When the state took custody of Danny, he was a cute seven-year-old. His mother had abandoned him, his extended family couldn't care for him, and his father was serving a long prison sentence. By the time the state made him available for adoption, almost three years had passed. Danny was a heavily medicated ten-year-old who had been kicked out of three foster homes, had a terrible school record, multiple diagnosed psychological disorders and a well-documented history of bed-wetting, fighting, compulsive stealing, food hoarding and lying.

While he was in the state's care, Danny never experienced life in a loving home or bonded successfully with a parent figure. Danny was described to me as "a 'thrownaway[2] kid' who needs a miracle." The more I learned about his background, the more I realized that without a miracle, he was doomed.

CHAPTER TWO

JAKE

For years I thought it would be impossible to become a dad because I was gay. Watching my friends and family have children was bittersweet. Though I was happy for them, it reminded me how much I wanted to be a father. I imagined myself holding my son or daughter, reading stories, singing, playing and laughing with my children the way my parents did with me.

During the 1990s, more and more gay men became parents. I started to believe that having a child might be possible. I told a friend who was a single parent that I wanted to become a dad.

"Why don't you get a dog first?" she suggested. "Kids can be a lot of work, and if you can't take care of a dog you certainly shouldn't adopt a child. At least you can take a dog to a shelter if it doesn't work out. Once you get a kid, you're stuck."

My business was thriving and I didn't have time to take care of a child or a dog, but I knew she was right. A few months later, I bought a Soft Coated Wheaten Terrier. Because his fur as a puppy was brown, I named him Rusty.

Two months after I brought Rusty home, I was offered a job with an Internet startup in California. It was 1999, technology was booming, and the stock options were going to be worth millions. All I had to do was abandon my dog, work 14 hours a day and turn my local business over to my partner. I decided that if the new company let me bring Rusty to work I'd do it, but they said pets weren't allowed. When I realized I had to abandon my dog to become financially successful I decided the price was too high. For the first time, I decided to pursue quality of life over earning money. I don't abandon children, friends, family or dogs.

My mom and dad met at Brigham Young University and married in 1958 in the Salt Lake City Mormon Temple. Three years later, they both started teaching on an Air Force base in Germany, where I was born in 1963. My parents wanted children, but pregnancy wasn't happening. I was the result of fertility doctor visits and prayers.

In 1964 we moved to Palo Alto, California, where my younger brother was born and my dad finished his doctorate at Stanford. Two years later, we moved to Ashland, Oregon and my other brother was born. In 1970 my dad accepted a teaching position at a university in Washington State, where my sister was born.

When I was one, my mom quit teaching to be a full-time mother. When I was four, we were both bored, so she taught me to read.

One of her techniques was writing a word like "LOOK" in frosting on a cookie. If I read the word, I got the cookie. Soon my ability to read was greater than the space she had to write in (it's hard to write "UNDERSTANDING" or "CALIFORNIA" in frosting), so we read books. We read, played, listened to records, laughed, cooked and cleaned house. I loved being with my mother and was delighted when my dad, an immigrant from Holland, came home and read us stories of Brownie Bear, the Dutch version of the British Rupert Bear.

In kindergarten I was placed in second-grade reading. In first grade, I was working beyond the class and after a few months the school moved me to second grade.

I hated the move. I was small for my age, and the older kids resented me. I learned that second-graders don't like first-graders showing them up.

After moving to second grade, I wasn't allowed to eat lunch with my first-grade friends. My new classmates often made me look bad at baseball, kickball, running and P.E. That wasn't hard; my coordination was below average, and I was more than a year younger than my classmates. I learned to hate sports, recess and going outside. My safety was found in classrooms, libraries and books.

In third grade, my teacher sent two bullies and me to an unsupervised textbook storage room for 15 minutes a day. My job was to "tutor" them. I was only seven. The eight- and nine-year-old bullies threatened to beat me up if I didn't do their assignments. When they learned I usually had money, they demanded I pay them to "protect" me. I hated myself for being weak, but I was little and didn't know what else to do.

In fourth and fifth grades, I avoided bullies. I often dodged sports or P.E. by pretending to be sick or injured. I didn't want to do anything I couldn't look good at.

In sixth grade, I fell in love with my locker partner. Though I didn't realize it then, I was gay. I adored him. We talked every day, ate lunch together, spent weekends sleeping over at each other's houses, listened to Casey Kasem's American Top 40, read science fiction and shared our dreams of the things we'd do when we were older. We were inseparable. I had never felt happier. This lasted three months.

In January he told me he was moving. I'd never felt such depression; I cried every night. I couldn't imagine living without him. My mom felt sorry for me and took me to Woolworth's to buy him a going-away gift. I gave it to him on his last day. He acted strangely, but I assumed he was traumatized by the move.

The next day I started to tear up when I saw his empty desk. I noticed a couple of boys laughing at me. At break I noticed a few other kids pointing at me and laughing. I assumed it was because they could tell I was sad. Still, I sensed something was wrong.

My class went to the choir room, and a half hour later my friend came in. I was elated. He was supposed to be gone. All my sadness vanished as quickly as bright light fills a dark room. I left my seat to talk to him. "What happened?" I whispered. "Why are you here? I'm so glad you're back!"

"I was never moving. I just had a dentist appointment." His voice echoed through the quiet classroom as his eyes informed me our friendship was over.

The music teacher told me to return to my seat and sing.

As the enormity of my friend's betrayal hit me, I saw our mutual friends laughing and clapping him on the back. They knew he wasn't moving—he just wanted to hurt me.

At that moment, at ten years old, I decided to use my head to make sure I was never hurt again and to seek revenge on anyone who ever hurt or betrayed me. That day I began sitting by myself at lunch. I avoided contact with kids at school and allowed only a little interaction with kids at church. I quit begging my parents to buy me fashionable jeans and shirts to wear to school—I didn't care what I wore—I knew I didn't fit in. At church I hung out with social misfits. I didn't want to grow close to anyone again.

In seventh grade, my parents and I were called into the school counselor's office.

"We're concerned about your son's grades. He is getting C's and D's, and he doesn't turn in assignments. His test scores, however, are among the highest in the school. We think he needs a psychiatrist."

The psychiatrist I saw for six months was physically

and emotionally intimidating. He asked questions about my feelings, sexual urges and my mother. When I didn't answer, he continuously stared at me. Sometimes five minutes passed without either of us speaking. I felt uncomfortable seeing him and added his name to my list of people to seek revenge on.

There were some older kids in my neighborhood who stole bicycles, burglarized houses and smoked marijuana. They made me feel welcome, and I hid from my parents what went on in their house. After a year of watching them get high, I tried marijuana. At 14, I discovered that getting high took my pain away. My anxiety, fear and shame all disappeared in the cloyingly sweet smoke. By 15, I was getting high every chance I could.

At 16, I refused to live at home and ended up in a group home for troubled boys. I stayed there almost six months before returning home in time to graduate from high school. That summer I joined the Army National Guard. After nine weeks of infantry boot camp at Fort Jackson, South Carolina, I started college. Other students introduced me to LSD, cocaine and shots of tequila. The next few years were a long spiral into the depths of addiction.

I don't know why I felt such intense pain. My parents did their best to love and support me. My siblings tried to befriend me, but my feelings were overwhelming. Drugs kept them at bay, but eventually the pain returned. I felt bad taking drugs, worse without them.

When I was 19 I was suspended from college for not going to class. I gathered hallucinogenic mushrooms and LSD and went alone to the woods and had a vision. I imagined myself being part of a totalitarian movement in the United States. Under the guise of security, protection and "the greater good of the country," I imagined fascism in America, with ethnic minorities and unpopular religions as scapegoats.

I felt there was potential for such a movement to go further than Hitler, as the propaganda in the United States in the 1980s was more sophisticated than 1930s Germany. I believed a fascist movement in the United States would ultimately fail, but destruction and chaos were my goal.

A few weeks later, I woke up in the middle of the night and heard a voice inside say: *You've gone far enough. You can kill yourself if you want, but this isn't your destiny. You need to stop now.*

I knew the voice was true. I decided to commit suicide rather than pursue my evil vision. Life as I knew it collapsed. I started stealing because drug dealers had quit giving me credit. I repeatedly forged my parents' checks and stole from them to buy drugs. When they finally turned me in (after forgiving me the first few times), I was convicted of forgery. I was sentenced to serve 30 days in work release. One day while serving my work-release sentence, I left my job early to get high with some friends. I became so intoxicated that I couldn't return to jail and was convicted of felony escape. My friends abandoned me, my family didn't trust me, and I almost died from an accidental overdose.

A judge offered me a choice between a year in substance-abuse treatment or a five-year prison sentence. When I learned I couldn't have cigarettes in treatment, I asked for prison so I could smoke. Eight months later I was paroled and spent the next four years bouncing in and out of drug-treatment centers, jails and 12-Step meetings. I couldn't stop thinking about using alcohol and other drugs.

Because of my addictions I couldn't hold a job. To support myself, I forged checks and stole money anywhere I could. To avoid returning to prison, I carefully planned my crimes and moved to different states frequently. I spent several years living under fake names and having little contact with my family. Though I didn't return to jail, the life I created was as confining as any prison.

I often thought of my grandma. I knew she unconditionally loved me. To avoid disappointing her, I lied and told her my life was going well. I didn't want to hurt her or the rest of my family by committing suicide so I killed myself slowly with my addictions.

I started attending 12-Step meetings sporadically. It was the only place I felt hope. I began working on my recovery with a sponsor and made friends with others struggling with the same addictions. It took me nine years from the time I attended my first meeting to finally quit using alcohol and all other drugs. I kept trying, even though I believed I would fail. I had never succeeded at growing up, and I had never learned to handle emotional pain.

The people in the meetings told me to "keep coming back," so I did. The only time I believed I might change was when I listened to other addicts and alcoholics share their stories of addiction, loss and redemption. Even though their background, age, gender, religion, sexual orientation, race and education were often different from mine, their experience of how addictions destroyed their lives was familiar. I believe listening to them saved my life.

My continuous abstinence from drugs and alcohol began in 1990. In the decades since then, I have healed my relationships with my family, stayed active in 12-Step programs, achieved financial success, embraced being gay, cleared all my criminal records and participated on committees and government boards to help homeless, mentally ill and addicted people. I became a productive, responsible, respected member of my community. Yet, when I see conscienceless, evil people seeking to control and destroy others, I understand them. I was once one of them.

By the time I was 40, I believed that I could become a father. Though I didn't know how it would work out or what it would look like, I told friends and family I intended to have a child. I read books about adoption and parenting and let my heart lead my head whenever a situation arose that could result in becoming a father.

Five years after the first of many attempts to become a dad, I met Danny.

CHAPTER THREE

THE BIRTH DAD

In 2003 my partner Terry and I decided to adopt a child. My instinct to parent was strong and I knew if I didn't find a way to become a dad I would regret it.

Our first step was to attend a weekend seminar on open adoption in Portland. When it was over, we knew we could spend $25,000 and wait many months, but we were excited.

A few months later a co-worker of Terry's told him she was pregnant and she'd like us to adopt her baby. We got her a therapist and a lawyer, paid her rent and made sure she had good medical care. A month later she quit her job, disappeared and used the rent money to pay for an abortion. Terry was devastated.

"Don't worry," I told him. "Remember what they said at the seminar. The only people who don't get kids are the ones who give up, and we aren't giving up. We just have to keep trying." Over the next few years several women offered to have babies for us, but Terry refused.

"I don't want to bring another kid into the world," he said. "I want to help a child already here." Although I was open to a biological child, Terry's desire ruled out having a baby with a friend or a surrogate mother. We prepared to register with an open-adoption agency and told everyone we were trying to adopt.

A friend, Franney Mack, who practices family law in Seattle, had a pregnant client whose four kids had been taken away because she was found an unfit mother. The mother wanted to give her child up for adoption at birth because if she didn't the state would take her baby away. We said we wanted to adopt the baby, finished our adoption home study and prepared to receive the child. After the baby was born, the mother decided to keep it and the state immediately placed the newborn in foster care. Terry was distraught and angry.

"Don't be upset, Terry," I encouraged him. "We can't be mad at a mother who chooses to keep her baby."

"I know, I know, but I am sick of this! We don't know if we're going to be parents in a month or if we will be waiting a year from now. I hate not knowing—it feels as if our lives are on hold."

"Why don't we try an international adoption? We know we'll eventually get a kid, and if something else works out we can do that instead."

Terry agreed, and I started researching. The only country I could find that allowed a single male to adopt was Vietnam, and none allowed foreign gay couples to become adoptive parents. I got an international adoption home study prepared and paid $5,000 to our new adoption agency. They said to expect to wait two years for a baby.

A year later I took an extended cruise in Asia with my mother and father. We spent three days in Vietnam and, while other passengers were touring museums and markets, we visited an orphanage. I had brought $1,000 worth of baby formula and food supplies for the orphanage and had a pleasant interview with the director. He seemed impressed that I brought my mom and dad and wanted to match me with a child immediately. But my file wasn't approved by the Vietnamese consulate yet, so he couldn't help. I emailed pictures from the orphanage to Terry, and we both got excited looking at the children.

In September, Franney called about another kid. She represented the boy's birthfather, who had spent the past eight years in prison.

"How old is the child?" I asked.

"He's nine. He's been in foster care more than two years, and his dad won't agree to termination of his parental rights until his son has a good home."

"What do you know about the kid?"

She was quiet a moment. "He has an extensive history of abuse and neglect. He's legally a special-needs kid, but all kids are when they're his age. He's been diagnosed with ADHD and takes medication, but that doesn't mean anything—the state likes to drug them so they're easier to handle. When I met him a few years ago, he was like many kids in the system—he's overmedicated, anxious and needs a parent to take care of him."

"I'll talk to Terry, but we're looking for an infant—we don't want an older kid with a bunch of issues."

"Will you consider meeting the dad? He'd love to talk to you. It would mean a lot to him."

"Does he know we're a gay couple?"

"Yes, and he's fine with that. He just wants a good home for his son."

Terry and I reluctantly agreed to drive to Seattle and meet the father. When we arrived at Franney's office, he was already sitting at her conference table. His fingers were dirty, and his nails were chipped. I could tell he had tried to scrub them; his hands said he did hard work. He stood up to greet us.

"Hi, I'm Stan."

"Hi, Stan," I replied. "My name is Jake, and this is Terry." We shook hands and sat down.

"I don't know how much you know about Danny," he began.

"Not much. Until now I didn't know his name."

"Well, he was with his mom for about a year. Then she left him with her mom—his grandma. She already left her other two twin girls with her mom when they was little. She don't really like kids after they start moving around and crawling. She likes little bitty infants. She's sorta slow in the head. I didn't even know I had a son till she came to the prison and said I should take a paternity test. I wanted to do right by him, but I was locked up and all. I took parenting classes and made recordings of me reading books to him, but I couldn't do much. Here's a picture of him."

He handed us a photo of a brown-haired six-year-old boy. I didn't feel any connection to the photo—it was just somebody else's kid.

"His mom and I got married while I was in the joint, and I started seeing Danny more regular. After we divorced, she gave up her rights to Danny to me and I sent him to live with my mom so he could get to know his other family…but that got really messed up. People were saying all sorts of shit—I mean stuff—about my mom and sister, how they beat him up and hurt him. When my mom got arrested over it, he ended up back with his other grandma until the state took him away. Her place was just a pigsty with cockroaches and bugs everywhere. She wasn't good at taking care of him at all!"

"How long ago was that?"

"Maybe two years ago. I don't want him in foster care. I'd like to raise him, but I just got out of prison, I don't have a permanent place to live and I work long hours in a wrecking yard. I can't take care of a little boy with Danny's needs."

"What are his needs?" Terry jumped in. Stan suddenly looked evasive.

"They say he's real active and don't sit still in school. He has a hard time focusing, but he's a good kid."

"Anything else?" I asked. His attorney gave him a pointed look.

"I heard he was suspended from school for beating up a kid on the bus, and he don't like foster care… I just want to do right by him. The court wants me to give him up, but I won't sign the papers unless there's a good home for him. I don't want him growing up in foster care."

"That's why you're meeting with us?" I asked.

"Yep. That's why. She said you're good people," he nodded toward his attorney. "And that you want to adopt a kid, so I asked to meet you and tell you about Danny."

"Thanks, Stan. We appreciate your considering us. We do want to adopt a child, and I respect that you're doing what you can to help Danny."

We talked a few more minutes, answered a few questions about our jobs, home and pets, and agreed to get back to him within a few weeks. Neither of us said much as we began the long drive home.

Finally, I couldn't stand the silence. "What do you think?"

"He seemed cute in the picture," Terry said cautiously.

"Most six-year-olds look cute in pictures. How old is he anyway?"

"I think Franney said he was nine." We were quiet. A troubled nine-year-old was very different from an infant. "I don't know, Jake. I just don't feel like this is a good idea for us. He already has a family, and it seems like he has quite a few problems. What do you think?"

"I think you're probably right." We turned up the music and made our way home. A few days later I called Franney and told her that though we appreciated meeting Stan, we didn't want to meet Danny. We were going to be matched with an infant in Vietnam soon, and we didn't want to adopt Danny—he was just too old.

Chapter Four

'Hallelujah'

Four months later, Terry and I broke up. We had been together eight years, and our separation was painful. He said the biggest reason he was leaving was his fear that I would leave him stuck at home with a baby when we adopted a child together. Most of my life I've been free of depression, so experiencing the end of a long relationship was heartbreaking and new.

I talked to my 12-Step sponsor and shared my conflict about adopting an infant as a single dad. "I don't think I can do it. You know how much time my business takes, and I'm constantly involved in recovery and community events. Besides, I don't even like infants that much; I find older kids more interesting. And I'm 45. If I take an infant, I'll be collecting Social Security when my kid turns 20!"

"Don't do it then," he suggested.

"But I've been trying to have a kid for five years! Any day I'll get a call saying 'We have a baby for you.' What do I say? 'I don't know?' They'll think I'm a flake!"

"Why don't you tell them you've had a personal situation arise and you can't accept a child for the next six months. By then you'll have had enough time to make a decision when you're not in so much pain."

His advice made sense. A week later I got the call. "Is this Jake?" The voice on the other end was enthusiastic. It was a gray, rainy day, and I was driving through downtown Seattle.

"Yes, it is."

"This is Susan from Grace International. I've got great news for you. We have a little girl that we'd like you to consider adopting!" For most prospective parents who have run the gauntlet of the adoption process, the call that there is a child is cause for celebration. I wanted to cry.

"That's great," I finally answered. "How old is she?"

"She's two and a half and in good health." I knew I needed to hang up the phone or I'd start crying.

"When do we need to get back to you? I am out of town and have to talk to my partner." The words escaped before I remembered that I should have said I was single now.

"Could you call by Monday? We need to move quickly. If you aren't interested, we have other couples who are. You're fine with a boy or a girl, right?"

"Yes, we are. I'll get back to you Monday. Thanks for the call." I tried to sound like a happy adoptive parent, but I felt like ramming my car into the concrete median.

Terry always wanted a girl, but my preference was a

boy. I like girls but know nothing about raising them. I worried about helping a daughter with her friendships with other girls, her boyfriends and her first menstrual cycle. I thought my experience growing up would be more useful with a boy.

But now, by saying yes, I'd be a father. *What if you never get another chance?* My inner voice was scared and convincing. But it felt wrong. My head kept wrestling with my desire to say adopt her, but my heart felt it was a mistake for both of us.

I left a message for Terry that we had been matched with a little girl. I hoped he would call, tell me he was sorry, move back home and then we could go to Vietnam and bring back our daughter together. He never called. On Monday, I followed my sponsor's advice and phoned the agency.

"Hi, Susan. It's Jake. I've spent all weekend agonizing over this, but I'm sorry. I need to pass."

"Is everything OK?"

"Yes, overall it is. The timing just isn't right. For about the next six months, I can't accept any matches. I want to leave my file active though. Can you do that?"

"Oh, sure. We can keep it open. I'll make a note. Just keep in touch with me and let me know if anything changes." When I hung up I felt sad, but I sensed this little girl needed to grow up in another family. It wasn't my destiny to be her dad, and I felt liberated saying no.

A few days later I received a voicemail from Franney.

"Danny's CASA[3] (court appointed special advocate) wants to talk to you. I told him you weren't interested in meeting Danny, but he still wants to call. May I give him your number?"

I ignored her message for a few days. I wanted to say no, but couldn't. When I was with Terry, he had strong feelings that we should refuse to consider having a biological kid, to use a surrogate mother or to raise the child of anyone we knew. Although I went along with Terry's decision for the sake of our relationship, I didn't feel the same. All along my journey to becoming a dad, I felt that however it unfolded would be right. Whether that meant adopting an infant, having a biological baby, raising a friend's child or adopting an older kid, my goal was to become a father, and I believed if I stayed open to all possibilities, my child would appear.

A week later I went to a k.d. lang concert in Seattle. When she started performing *Hallelujah*, an intense feeling moved through me.

"*I've heard there was a secret chord...* " As she started to sing, I was filled with a connection to love greater than I'd ever experienced. The lyrics moved me as tears fell down my face. I no longer felt I was at a concert; I was in the presence of sacred beauty.

You have to take him, said a calm, wise inner voice.

Take who?

Danny. He's your destiny. He's your son. I wanted to object and say no. But although I knew I could ignore it, I couldn't deny that the voice was true. As the music continued, a surge of déjà vu struck me so powerfully I was nauseated. I felt that in some other life or at some other time I had said no to being a dad.

I won't make that mistake again! In the intensity of my fierce intention, something clicked. My tears transformed to smiles of resignation as I was swept in a current of relentless love. *I'll take him.* There was no answer.

"*Hallelujah, Hallelujah, Hallelujah, Hallelujah.*" As the final notes of the song ended, I knew that life as I knew it was over. But I felt proud. I passed this test.

The next day, I let Franney know she could give Danny's CASA my number. Despite my willingness, I hoped he wouldn't call. The memory of the song was fading fast.

CHAPTER FIVE

THE CASA

"Hi. My name is Mike. I'm Danny's CASA. Do you have a moment to talk?"

"What's a CASA?"

"It stands for court appointed special advocate. I was appointed to serve as Danny's guardian ad litem. CASAs are the eyes and ears of the court."

I was in Los Angeles at a 12-Step service conference. A month had passed since the concert, and I had tried to convince myself that my experience during *Hallelujah* was all in my imagination.

"I've got a few minutes. How can I help you?"

"I wanted to talk about Danny. Are you still interested in adoption?"

"I never was really interested in adopting him. My partner and I separated five months ago, and he wanted a baby. I was matched with a little girl in Vietnam last month, but I turned her down because I don't have enough time to be a single dad to an infant."

"What about to a ten-year-old?"

I paused a moment. "I guess I feel more capable of parenting a ten-year-old than I do parenting an infant, but Danny has so many problems I don't think I can do much for him."

"There's something you need to know. Most older kids in the foster-care system like Danny have lots of labels. But they usually aren't near as bad as they look on paper. I'm not saying these kids are easy—they will test you— but most of their problems are from not having good families of their own. Danny needs someone he can count on. He needs a permanent, loving home. Without that, he'll bounce in and out of foster homes, get caught in the juvenile-justice system, drop out of school and probably end up in prison or homeless. I can't promise that you're a good match for him, but I'd like to come meet you."

"Why me?"

"You are the only prospect I can find in his file, and I don't like giving up on any of my kids."

"You know I live in Anacortes, right?"

"Yes, I know that."

"And you're willing to drive from Tacoma just to talk to me?"

"Yes, I'll come up on a Friday night after work."

I laughed. "You know that could take three or four hours with traffic?"

"It takes what it takes. Besides I have a daughter in Everett I can visit."

"If you're that committed to meeting me, I'll do it, but I think you're wasting your time." We set a date but, as our appointment grew near, I regretted my decision. I wasn't going to adopt a troubled ten-year-old from Tacoma.

The night of our meeting I came home from work early and straightened up the house. When Mike arrived, my dog Rusty was more enthusiastic about meeting him than I was. Rusty views every stranger as a potential friend.

Mike spent an hour asking about my life. He looked in my fridge, closets, bedrooms and garage. Finally, he started talking about Danny.

"Danny is an active, likeable kid. He struggles with impulsivity, and he wants a family of his own. He has twin sisters in foster care who live with their great-aunt. They don't see each other much. He likes baseball and skateboarding."

"Where does he live now?"

"He was in his last foster home almost two years. It's a home meant for a 30 days or less stay. It wasn't a good place for him."

"He lived in a 30-day foster home for two years?" I asked incredulously. "Why?"

"Because of his behavioral issues—which I don't think are all that severe—the state couldn't find him another home. His aunt considered taking him, but her house doesn't have enough bedrooms to meet the licensing requirements. Right now he's in a short-term specialized foster home because his old foster mom kicked him out of her house."

"Why did she kick him out?"

"She bought a new Cadillac, and Danny vandalized it. She called the police and kicked him out."

"Do you know why he vandalized it?"

"I don't. He was angry, upset—he was told a week before that he had to move out soon so maybe he wanted to leave right away."

"What kind of specialized foster home is he living in now?"

"It's a BRS home, which means behavioral rehabilitation services. It's a foster-care program for the most difficult kids. Look, I'm not going to lie to you. On paper Danny looks terrible. None of our interventions have worked. What Danny needs is permanency—a family of his own. I believe if he gets that, most of his problems will go away. You would still have some problems, but all parents have problems with their kids. It's part of being a parent." I noticed he was speaking as if I were taking Danny.

"What do you want from me?"

"I want you to meet him and see what you think." His entire visit had built up to this request. He stared quietly, waiting for my reply.

I didn't want to meet Danny. I was afraid. The more I thought about becoming his dad the more fear I felt. I was scared I wasn't capable of being a good father and that I would fail miserably in a misguided effort to save a troubled ten-year-old boy.

Don't do it! You have no business meeting Danny. Say good-bye! The voice of fear inside was loud and persuasive.

"Mike, I really appreciate your coming up but—"

Before I could finish my sentence, I remembered how I felt listening to k.d. lang. *What does Hallelujah mean? Praise God? What is a spiritual experience? Did I have one? Does my growth and development depend on following my heart?* I knew I could listen to my fear and turn away from Danny, or I could accept the love and connection I felt for him listening to k.d. lang sing.

"—but it might be a week or two before I can meet him." Mike looked delighted as he shook my hand.

"I knew it was important to come talk to you. I could feel it. Thanks for agreeing to meet him. I need to talk to his social worker, but I'll get back to you next week with some dates." Rusty kept licking Mike's hand as he followed him outside.

What have I done! I felt anxious. My stomach was uneasy and tense. For a long time, I didn't call anyone. I didn't know what to say. I sat on my couch idly scratching Rusty's ears. Finally, I called my parents. My mom answered on the second ring.

"Hello?" It was late and she sounded worried.

"Hi, Mom. It's Jake."

"Oh, hi!" she sounded relieved.

"Mom, do you remember that ten-year-old I told you about a few months ago—the one in foster care in Tacoma?

"You mean the boy that had all those troubles?"

"Yeah, him." She waited for me to say more but I was silent.

"Yes, I remember…"

"Well, his CASA was just here for a few hours. He wants me to meet Danny."

"Do you think that's a good idea?"

"Probably not. I don't know. Maybe." I was embarrassed to tell her about my experience at the k.d. lang show. "I've decided to meet him—I haven't committed to anything— and I'd like you to come with me."

"Sure, I'll come. When are you going?"

"I don't know. Soon. I'll have a date early next week."

"Let me know as soon as you can. Your father and I have a concert next Thursday, and we have a church dinner Saturday."

"It probably won't be a weekend. I'll let you know soon. Thanks, Mom."

"You're welcome. Do you want to talk to your father?"

"No, you can tell him."

"OK. Goodnight, Jake. We love you."

"I love you too." As I hung up, I wondered if she thought I sounded crazy. *What am I doing? Am I crazy?* There was no answer.

I didn't sleep well that night. I still felt anxious. The

next morning I wished the previous evening was a bad dream. But Mike had left his business card next to my coffeemaker. It was all real; I was meeting Danny soon.

Chapter Six

Watch and Learn

"Who's going to be at this meeting?" my mom asked. We were driving to Tacoma to meet Danny.

"Let's see. There will be his CASA, his case manager, his social worker, her supervisor, his counselor, a nurse and probably a few others."

"That sounds like a lot of people. Will Danny be there?"

"No, we see all of them at their office at 11, then we meet Danny at a restaurant around noon." I glanced at my watch. It was 9:30, and we still had 75 miles to go.

When we arrived, a woman came out to greet us. She looked familiar but I couldn't place her. "Hi, Jake. Remember me?"

"I'm sorry, I'm not sure where I know you from."

"I'm Sienna. I was assigned to you at Grace International Adoption."

"That's right! That's why I didn't recognize you. We talked a lot on the phone but met just once. What are you doing here?"

"I'm Danny's counselor. After I left Grace, I got an internship here. I'm taking you to meet him after our meeting. I'm glad you're considering adopting him." The coincidence was stunning. What were the odds that the woman who prepared my Vietnam adoption file was now Danny's counselor?

"Mom, this is Sienna. She worked for the agency that Terry and I used for Vietnam. Remember those orphanages we visited on the cruise?"

"Hi, Sienna. That was quite a day in Vietnam. Some of those kids broke my heart."

"I know. Their stories are just gut wrenching." She turned toward me, "I've been telling everyone what a great guy you are. We're so excited you're interested in Danny."

She led us to a conference room, and we went around the table introducing ourselves. Sienna led off. "I'm Danny's counselor. Danny is a charming little boy. He loves baseball and playing outside." As she kept talking about what a wonderful kid Danny was, I felt like I was listening to a television evangelist. She said nothing about his challenges. The more she overemphasized his strengths and ignored his weaknesses, the more it felt like a snow job.

A nurse talked about Danny's mental-health diagnosis and his current psychiatric medications. His state social worker, Louise, took the same tack as Sienna. It began to feel as if I were buying an overpriced ten-year-old Buick.

"May I ask a few questions?" I asked. "I understand that Danny has some sexually aggressive behaviors. Is that true?" A few heads nodded. "Can someone tell me what they are?" No one spoke.

"He had an incident at school," his case manager, Sally, finally said. "What happened is that Danny unzipped his zipper, stuck his finger through it and moved his finger up and down to simulate his penis. He also told a girl it was her job to have sex with him. He was suspended for both."

"Is there anything else?"

"Yes, there was an incident when he first entered foster care. Danny kissed a six-year-old girl who lived at the same foster home. When he was asked why, he said, 'because she's my sister so I kissed her good night.'"

"That's it? A kiss and wriggling his finger through his zipper?"

"Foster children aren't allowed to do those things," the state supervisor interjected. "We are required by law to investigate whenever children have possible sexual contact."

"But he is a little boy! Lots of boys wriggle their fingers through their zippers. I probably did it myself at his age. It's hardly sexually aggressive behavior. I did worse than that when I was six, playing doctor with the neighbor girl in her basement." My mom smiled and nodded in agreement.

"I have a few questions," my mom said. "Can anyone tell me how Danny is doing in school?"

"He has an IEP that's mostly for behavioral issues," Sally replied.

"What's an IEP?" I asked.

"An Individualized Education Program. Danny struggles in school. He desperately wants attention, so he'll do almost anything to get people to notice him. Academically he's inconsistent. In testing he sometimes performs far below grade level. Other times his performance is fine. The school is concerned about what to do with him, and the vice-principal and I have spent a lot of time developing strategies to keep him in a regular classroom."

"How is his reading?" My mom asked.

"He can read, but it's below grade level," Sally turned toward me, "What kind of school would you put him in? Danny could use a Montessori school or an environment where he could move around and get lots of personal attention."

"I have no idea what school he would attend. I'm meeting him for the first time and don't know if I'll see him again." Sally met my eye, and I felt a sense of mutual respect. I admired her advocacy for Danny, and though others in the room were fawning over me, her focus was on what was best for him.

"I guess it's time for you to go meet him," Louise said brightly.

"Does he have any idea why he's meeting me?"

"Yes, I told him you were thinking about adopting him."

"Really? What if I don't ever see him again? Wouldn't it have been better to meet casually? I don't want to disappoint him, and I have no idea if I am interested in adopting him."

"Well, that's what he knows," Louise shrugged.

Since Mike's visit I'd imagined many times my first meeting with Danny. I convinced myself that the instant I saw him I would know if he was the right kid for me. In my car outside the restaurant, I watched Sienna accompanying a small boy wearing a Seattle Mariners baseball cap and matching jacket.

That's not your son. Drive away! The voice in my head was loud and demanding. Before I could react, my mom said, "I think I see them. We'd better go in." I nodded and followed her.

Standing in the lobby was a four-foot, six-inch, 70-pound ten-year-old. His fingernails were chewed and bloody. He looked too skinny, and with his crew cut he reminded me of a concentration-camp prisoner. His beautiful brown eyes betrayed his sadness.

"Jake, this is Danny," Sienna said.

"Hi, Danny." I held out my hand.

"Hi," he said shyly. I felt thick calluses on his little palms.

"I brought something for you, Danny," he looked interested. "It's a Mariners baseball cap that lights up. I'll show you how it works." I turned it on, and lights flashed blue and green around the Mariners'"M".

"That's tight!" He turned it on and off and adjusted it to fit his head. I watched our reflection in the mirror behind him. It looked odd. The whole experience felt surreal. *What the hell am I doing here?*

"This is my mom. She wanted to meet you too."

"Hi, Danny. It's nice to meet you."

"Hi." He couldn't keep eye contact with either of us. He whispered something to Sienna.

"OK," she told him, "but only one game." She handed him quarters, and he disappeared into the video-game room. "He can be kind of shy."

"That's understandable," my mom said. "This is a scary situation for any kid." His game ended and our table was ready. I felt no connection to him and thought this was the last time I'd see him. As we walked toward our table, Danny pointed at a picture.

"Mickey Mouse. Cool!" Although Danny couldn't have known it, I love Mickey Mouse, and Walt Disney is one of my heroes. Some of my best memories with my family were our annual summer trips to California to visit relatives and go to Disneyland.

There's a connection—he likes Mickey Mouse.

Any kid might say Mickey Mouse is cool. It doesn't mean you should be his father! As I listened to the debate in my head, I remembered that the scared voice is usually loud and the wise voice is harder to hear.

We sat down and Danny started furiously coloring his menu. Within seconds he broke his crayon and pouted. After we ordered our lunch he asked, "Do you want to play a game?"

"Sure," I replied.

"You can go first," he pointed to the tic-tac-toe drawing on his kids' placemat. I marked an X and he made an O. In a few moves I beat him. "Want to play again?" he asked.

"Sure, but this time you go first." I won again. Either he was really stupid or he was letting me win. "Danny?" His eyes jerked up. "Are you letting me win?" He gave a shy smile, but a hint of playfulness escaped his eyes.

"Maybe…" he grinned. For a moment he felt genuine, and I smiled back. Our food arrived. As we started to eat, Danny began making odd noises. Sienna tried to quiet him.

"Why are you making those weird sounds, Danny?"

"This is my french-fry noise!" It sounded like he was trying to sing while gulping milk.

"Do you have any other noises?" I asked, trying to assure Sienna I wasn't concerned.

"Lots! I have noises for everything. I have a hamburger noise, a pizza noise, an apple noise—here's the hamburger one." He honked his nose. The ladies at the table near us glared.

"Danny," Sienna said, "can you please save your noises until we are outside?"

"OK," he replied as he stuffed more french fries into his mouth.

"Danny," my mom asked, "can you please quit kicking me? You've been doing it most of the time we've been here, and it doesn't feel good." He hung his head and didn't say anything.

Finally he muttered, "Sorry."

After we finished eating, Sienna tried to start a conversation. "Danny, Jake travels a lot. He's been all over the world. Can you tell Danny some of the countries you've been to?"

"Sure, I've been to Holland—that's where my dad was born. I've been to Egypt and saw the pyramids. I've been to Peru, China, India, Kenya, Vietnam and quite a few other places."

"Have you been to Afghanistan?" Danny asked loudly.

"Uh, no, I haven't been there. Why?" He shrugged and looked down.

"Danny," Sienna asked, "if you could go any place in the world, where would that be?"

"That's easy. Disneyland! Yea! Disneyland!" He shouted. I noticed we were attracting attention from the other diners again.

"That's one of my favorite places too, Danny. I hope you go there someday." I was careful not to say I hoped to take him.

"Danny," Sienna asked, "you have some questions for Jake, don't you?" He looked away from her but nodded his head yes. "Would you like to ask him those questions?" He shook his head no. "Danny, we practiced this earlier today. Remember? Could you please ask just one of the questions we practiced?"

Without looking up he softly asked, "If you adopt me, will I get to see my sisters?"

"Danny, you have two older sisters, don't you?" He looked up and nodded. "What are their names?"

"Ashley and Emily," he sounded young and shy.

"How old are they?"

"Almost 16," he whispered.

"You must love them a lot, huh?" He nodded as tears began to fall. "You miss them, don't you?" He nodded again as he quietly cried. "Danny, I don't know your sisters, but I'm sure they're wonderful. Anyone lucky enough to adopt you should let you see your sisters. They'll always be part of your family, and family is important. That's why my mom is here—I was scared to meet you alone. I have two younger brothers and a younger sister, and I love them very much. So, yes, I think whoever adopts you should let you see your sisters."

"Does that answer your question, Danny?" Sienna asked. He nodded as he wiped his eyes and nose with the collar of his T-shirt. "Can you ask one of your other questions?"

"OK," he asked with a little more confidence, "If you adopt me, where would we live?"

"I live in Anacortes. It's about 100 miles north of here on the ocean, near the Canadian border."

"What kind of house do you have?"

"I have two houses. One is a small house on the ocean that I live in during the summer, and the other is on five acres in the woods. There's a creek that runs behind the backyard, and it's surrounded by trees. It's a nice house— you'd have your own room and lots of places to play outside." I quit talking as I realized I was describing my home as if I wanted him to live there. I still didn't plan to see him again.

After lunch, Sienna suggested we walk across the parking lot to the mall. When we got outside, Danny asked, "Where's your car?" I pointed to my Mustang Cobra. "Whoa, that's tight!"

"Have you been in a Mustang before?"

"No, but I want to. Can we? Please?"

Sienna agreed and we got in. Danny kept rolling his rear window up and down, putting his hand and head out the window and playing with the rear-seat DVD screen.

At the mall, Danny went directly to a video-game store that allowed kids to play if their parents are with them. After ten minutes, Sienna made him quit. "Hey, since you might be my dad, can you buy me a baseball glove?"

"No, I can't. They're expensive, and I don't even know if they have them here."

"They do have them! I know they do! C'mon! I'll show you where they are," he started dragging me toward a store.

"Danny, you can't ask Jake to buy you things," Sienna said.

"Why not? If he's going to be my dad, he can buy me a baseball glove!" He glared at her.

"Not this time, Danny. Sorry."

He let go and turned away mad.

My mom wanted to use the mall washroom next to

the food court before we drove home. "Are you all right watching Danny for a few minutes while I use the bathroom too?" Sienna asked.

"Sure, go ahead." It was my first time alone with him.

"Want something to eat?" Danny asked. His anger over the baseball glove disappeared as quickly as it arose.

"What've you got?"

"Come with me," he said slyly. He approached a food-court restaurant and came back with two chicken samples on toothpicks.

"That was good. Thanks, Danny." I got up to leave.

"WAIT!" he shouted. "We have to get the good ones!"

"What are the good ones?"

"You'll see. Watch and learn," he gave a conspiratorial grin as he raced to get more samples. I started laughing. Telling me to "watch and learn" was like the Artful Dodger in Oliver Twist offering to teach Fagan how to steal.

As I watched him return with the food for me, a genuine connection to Danny emerged. A wave of compassion for him struck me. I wanted to take him home, tuck him in bed at night and comfort him when he cried. I wanted to teach him, guide him, protect him and love him. I wanted to be his dad.

CHAPTER SEVEN

FIRST VISIT

The next morning Danny's social worker, Louise, called, "How was your lunch with Danny?"

"It was good. I told him I'd see him again soon."

"Great! When would you like to do that?"

"Next weekend. I'd like to take him to lunch and a movie."

"That should be fine. I'll arrange it with his foster parents."

Later that day Sally, Danny's case manager, called. "So now that you have spent some time with him, what do you think?"

"He seems like a nice kid. Kind of hyper, really anxious, but I like him. Have you seen his fingernails? He bites them past the skin!"

"Yes, I've noticed. He is a great kid, but he has a lot of anxiety. I think many of his issues will go away if he finds a loving home. Do you have any experience working with special-needs kids?"

"No, I don't. I know Danny's had a tough life, but I don't know much about him. Has he been physically abused, sexually abused? What's his story?"

She paused. "Danny was physically abused by his paternal grandmother. She regularly beat and tortured him. It got so bad that she was arrested. At his other grandma's he was neglected. Her house was filthy, there were issues like no hot water, and she let unsafe people come around him. Danny needs an extraordinarily patient and understanding caregiver. He will test you. He hasn't ever had a mom or dad take care of him. His mom abandoned him when he was less than a year old. His dad has been in prison most of Danny's life. His maternal grandma wants to care for him and visits him regularly, but there are too many concerns to allow him to live with her. His twin sisters are living with a great-aunt, but that hasn't worked out as an option for him either."

"What do think is wrong with him?"

"He's impulsive and doesn't seem to learn from his mistakes. It's kind of like he has a Swiss cheese brain. Some things stick, and some things just pass right through. He steals and lies constantly, but it seems to be mostly for attention. Those of us that work with Danny like him—he's pleasant and eager to please. We haven't been able to find a good home for him because of his behavior. His school wants to place him in a self-contained classroom for disturbed children, but his teacher wants to keep him in her class."

"Does he have a learning disability?"

"Probably, but it's hard to tell. His testing is all over the map, and his IEP (Individual Education Plan) is for behavioral issues. He disrupts the class constantly—he makes funny noises, eats things that aren't food and does anything he can to get attention."

"I appreciate you sharing this with me, but it almost feels like you're trying to talk me out of adopting him. Do you think I'm a bad fit for Danny?"

"I don't know if you are a good fit or a bad fit, but I don't want to see Danny grow attached to you unless you want to adopt him. He'll be devastated if he's abandoned again, and I don't think you have any idea of what you're getting into."

I chuckled, "You're right about that. I don't have a clue what I'm getting into. That's why I appreciate talking to you. It feels like Louise wants me to take Danny so she can get him off her caseload, and I don't know if I'm up to being his dad. In a way this whole idea seems foolish to me. When I started trying to become a parent I wanted an infant. This may sound strange but my head keeps telling me I'm crazy to consider taking Danny, but my heart keeps saying do it. I don't know what I'm going to do—I really don't. But I promise I'll do my best not to hurt him. If you see me doing anything you think is bad for him, please tell me."

"You can call anytime. Good luck with your next visit. I'll be anxious to hear how it goes."

My head felt overwhelmed by the reasons I shouldn't

take Danny. Adopting him would hurt my business and take time away from things I enjoy. Single parenting any kid is difficult, and adopting him meant my personal freedom would disappear.

But for all those concerns, my heart sang: *Take him. He needs you. If not you, who? If not now, when?* Some decisions can't be made by reason—they are an intuitive leap of faith. Adopting Danny would never be a logical choice.

The next weekend I drove to his foster home. I was early, but Danny was watching out the front window, excited as a six-year-old waiting for relatives to arrive Christmas Day. As I walked up the front porch, he started jumping.

His foster mother opened the door, and Danny came running full force toward me. He jumped up, threw his arms around my neck and yelled, "Hi, Dad!"

"Uhhh, hi, Danny. How are you?"

"I'm great! Let's go to the movies, Dad!" He started tugging me away from the house.

It was the first time anyone called me Dad. I felt like someone punched me in the gut. I wanted to drive home and pretend this wasn't happening. It was as uncomfortable as being asked to get married on a first date.

Danny sat in the passenger seat, impatient to leave. He tried every switch and knob in the car; he was constantly moving. Danny was well behaved during the first hour of the film, but then he began making inappropriate noises, laughing loudly when the theater was quiet and doing all he could to attract attention to himself. I wasn't successful keeping him focused on the movie. As the show ended the theme song caught my ear. The lyrics described a child who finally discovers his true home.

I felt an echo of the feeling I experienced listening to k.d. lang sing *Hallelujah*. Watching Danny while listening to the music, I knew that a loving force was guiding us toward each other.

When I brought Danny back to his foster home, he grabbed me and started bawling. His tears smeared my cheeks and arms as I tried to make him let go.

"Please don't leave me, Daddy. Don't leave me. PLEASE don't leave me," he wailed. I had no choice. He had to stay at his foster home. My heart went out to him as I witnessed his fear of my abandoning him.

"Danny, Danny," I murmured, "I'll see you soon. I promise I'll be back. I'll try to come next weekend and we can go to another movie, OK?"

"OK," he sniffled. "You promise?"

"Yes, buddy, I promise."

"Pinky swear?" He held his crooked pinky toward me. I touched our fingers together.

"Yes, pinky swear."

"I love you, Daddy! I love you! You're the best daddy in the world!" he screamed as his foster mom closed the door between us.

"Bye, Danny." Part of me wanted to tell him I loved him, but I couldn't do it; the words wouldn't come. He watched me start my car, back out of the driveway and get on the road. I glanced back as his foster home disappeared from view. He was standing with his nose and hands pressed against the porch window sobbing.

The next day I wrote a long email to his team of caregivers and social workers. I said I intended to adopt Danny and it was important he come live with me as soon as possible. I never wanted to return Danny to a foster home again. Watching his terror that I might abandon him tore my heart. I had started to think of him as my son, and I wanted to bring him home.

Chapter Eight

First Overnight

Two weeks later I got permission to have Danny for an overnight visit. I picked him up about one o'clock on a warm Sunday, and we headed to Anacortes with our windows down, sunroof open and radio blaring. A mile from his foster home Danny got upset.

"We have to go back!"

"What's wrong, Danny?"

"I forgot my skateboard! I really need it! I need to show it to you. Please. We have to go back. Can you just do a U-turn? Please!"

He was so anxious and insistent I turned around. Danny ran inside and seconds later burst into the car. "Isn't this tight! I painted it myself with permanent markers." In Danny's arms was a three-foot-long, two-inch by six-inch roughly cut board that would look more at home at a construction site than beneath a child's skateboarding shoes. He had attached wheels to the bottom.

"Wow, Danny. I've never seen a skateboard before that was really a wood board. You made that yourself?"

"Yep," his eyes were full of pride. I thought about the courage it took for Danny to ride his plank of wood around other kids who had store-bought skateboards.

As we drove north, he asked about the lakes we saw, the mountains in the distance and if we were almost there yet. Near Mount Vernon, Danny noticed Mount Baker glistening in the afternoon sun. "What's that?"

"That's Mount Baker. It's one of my favorite places in the world. When I was a kid I loved going skiing there. How does Anacortes seem different to you from Tacoma, Danny?"

"Well, there are a lot more trees...and that's a really cool mountain."

I laughed. "That's exactly what I was thinking. Hey, Danny?"

"Yes."

"There's something I want you to know about me."

"What?"

"I'm gay."

"Yeah, right," he laughed. He thought I was teasing.

"Danny, I really am gay."

"Really?" he looked upset and scrunched his face in disgust.

"Yes, really. I don't want too many secrets between us, and all of my friends know I'm gay. You might even meet my ex-partner, Terry.

"Oh..." I could tell he was shocked.

"Danny, I might be gay, but I can still be a good dad.

The reason I'm having you spend the night tonight and meet Rusty is so we can find out if we like each other enough to create a family together. If you choose me to be your dad, some kids might tease you because I'm gay, and I'm sorry about that, but I'd rather adopt you and have you be my son than leave you in foster care."

"I just thought all gay people were bad," he answered. "And I know you aren't bad."

"Yeah, some people think that. But it isn't true. Look, here's the turn to my house."

As we reached the end of the driveway, Danny turned to me excitedly. "There's a boat! This house is tight."

"Where do you want to start, Danny? Inside or out?" I opened the front door of the house to let Rusty outside.

"Outside!" he yelled, running. "Is that Rusty?" Without waiting for an answer he shouted, "C'mon, Rusty, chase me!" Rusty, my well-mannered nine-year-old dog, happily obliged. "Does Rusty really do what you tell him?"

"Yes, he does. Rusty!" I commanded. "Come!" Rusty trotted toward me. When he was ten feet away, I shouted, "Down!" Rusty dropped instantly.

Danny giggled, "Cool. Will he do that for me?"

"Yes, he'll do that and more. Rusty is smart—you don't even have to talk to him—he knows sign language."

"Really! Really! Show me!" Danny started jumping, and Rusty eyed him nervously.

"I will, but you need to stand still. It confuses Rusty when you move fast." Danny quit jumping but began tapping his fingers on his jeans. "Watch this, Danny." I extended my hand horizontally in front of my chest and thrust it down. Rusty dropped to a perfect down stay.

"Whoa! Cool!"

"Rusty knows how to get up too." I made a thumbs-up motion with my right hand, and Rusty moved to a sitting position.

"That's so tight!"

"It gets better. Watch." I alternated up and down hand signals. Rusty followed perfectly: dropping, sitting, dropping, and sitting. "I call this doggy push-ups."

Danny laughed. "Can I try?"

"Sure, you can try later."

"Can I get in the boat?" He started climbing the ladder before I could answer.

"Sure," we both climbed up to the bridge of my old cabin cruiser. It has upper seating for six and a small fo'c'sle with a head, galley and sleeping area.

"What's down there?" Danny pointed toward the fo'c'sle door.

"The kitchen, bathroom and a place to sleep."

"Tight," he said as he moved toward the door. "ARRRRRGGGGHHH! NO! NO! NO! GET AWAY!" Danny was screaming and jumping. Rusty ran in circles, barking and trying to figure out what was wrong.

I rushed to Danny, "What's wrong! What happened?" He could barely speak through his sobbing.

"A...a...a...spider! Ohhh...LOOK!" He pointed to

a six-inch spiderweb. In the center was a brown spider slightly larger than a sunflower seed. Danny's reaction was worthy of a tarantula.

I remembered Danny grew up in a house infested with cockroaches, insects and spiders. "You're pretty scared of spiders, huh, Danny?"

"I hate them," he sniffled. "Can we get out of the boat now? Please?" He looked four years old.

"Sure." We climbed down the ladder, went in the house and he started exploring.

"Can we start upstairs and then go downstairs?"

"Sure." We headed up with Rusty leading the way.

"Is this my room?" he asked as we entered the master bedroom.

"No, that's my room," I led him to the guest room. "If you live here, this will be your room." Rusty licked his hand as Danny scratched his muzzle.

"I like it, Dad. Where am I sleeping tonight?" His caseworker told me Danny often wets the bed. The guest bed had a down comforter; I didn't want Danny sleeping on it. "I thought you could stay in the TV room downstairs on an inflatable mattress with Rusty. Would you like that?"

"OK." He didn't sound enthusiastic though Rusty perked up at hearing his name.

After we ate some pizza, Danny decided to take a bath. Because we just met, it felt awkward to offer to help him with his bath.

"When you're ready, Danny, just turn off the water and get in. There are jets that feel good if you push the button.

Are you going to be OK?" He nodded. "All right, just call if you need anything." A few minutes later he came running down the stairs dripping wet and crying.

"What happened, Danny?"

"My foot got stuck in the bathtub and it wouldn't come out," he sobbed. "It tried to suck up my foot! I hate that tub!"

"Do you want to try again?"

"Yes, if you get in with me. Please?" A vision flashed through my mind of trying to explain to his social worker why I took a bath with Danny.

"No, the bathtub is too small for both of us." We watched TV, and soon I realized it was 10:30.

"Danny, you need to go to bed. Your bedtime is 8:30, and it's now 10:30."

"Nine."

"What?"

"My bedtime is nine," his eyes never left the television.

"Either way, it's time for bed." I turned off the TV. He glared at me a moment, suppressed his anger and started getting ready for bed.

"I think my tooth is coming out!" During dinner Danny informed me his last baby tooth was loose. "When I lost my teeth in the foster home, my foster mom said the tooth fairy ran out of money. If I lose my tooth here, will the tooth fairy come?"

"Danny, if you lose your tooth here, I guarantee the tooth fairy will come."

"Good!" We went to the bathroom, and I looked

closely at his molar. I wiggled it, and though it was loose it seemed pretty secure. "Do you have a hammer? I think I can knock it out!"

"No, Danny. If you can take it out with your tongue or fingers, that's fine, but we aren't going to knock your tooth out with a hammer."

"Please! I really need it out tonight," he sounded desperate. "I want the tooth fairy to come!" He gave me the best begging look he could muster.

"No, you have to do it on your own. No pliers, no hammers—just your tongue or your fingers."

"What's that noise!" he yelled, startling Rusty and me.

"What's what noise?"

"That bell ringing…"

"That's a grandfather clock that I got from my grandma."

"Can you turn it off, please?"

I turned off all the clocks, but living on five rural acres there are lots of sounds: coyotes, dogs, a creek, and the wind blowing through the trees. Danny was scared of them all.

"Can I please sleep in your room? I'm afraid to stay downstairs."

"I guess, Danny, but I snore so that might keep you awake…" I hoped he would change his mind.

"I don't mind," he carried his inflatable bed to my bedroom floor and put it next to Rusty's bed.

"Dad, do you sleep with the lights off?"

"Yes, I do. Why? Would you like some lights on?"

"Yes, please." I grabbed a few nightlights and plugged them in.

"How's that?"

"Can we have some more lights please?" I turned my overhead bedroom light on.

"Is that better?"

"Yep, but I don't think I'll sleep tonight... I usually don't sleep the first night in a new house. Once at respite I didn't sleep for two days. They had a furnace by my bedroom, and it scared me. I asked them to turn it off, but they said if they did we'd be cold in the morning so I just didn't sleep." I believed him. Whenever he hears an unfamiliar sound, his whole body tenses up and he looks terrified. "I know! I'll drink some warm milk and then I'll go to sleep, Dad."

I heated some milk (first it was too cold, then it was too hot), and we sat in the kitchen waiting for it to settle at a comfortable temperature. "May I have a cookie?" My mom had given me some homemade chocolate-chip cookies for him.

"No, it's too late. Just the milk." We went back upstairs. It was well after midnight. "Are you getting sleepy yet, Danny?"

"No, but I think if we play my story I could go to sleep."

"What story is that?"

"*The Emperor's New Clothes*. It's in my CD case." The CD case was in his backpack, which he left downstairs. Since he was frightened to go downstairs alone, Rusty and

I went with him. Rusty looked at me confused. *Who is this kid and why aren't we sleeping?*

"Why don't we grab your whole backpack, Danny? That way if you need anything else we'll have it." I put the CD on, and we started listening to a 40-minute version of *The Emperor's New Clothes* as narrated by a smart aleck moth with a Brooklyn accent. With my bedroom light on, the CD playing and Danny finally lying on his bed, I was hopeful I might finally get some sleep.

"I think my tooth is coming out!"

"Let's see, Danny," I sighed. "Come on in the bathroom." We turned on the lights, and Danny wiggled his tooth.

"It's out! See!" In his hand was a small primary molar. Blood gushed out of his mouth. "Oh no, I'm bleeding! I hate blood!"

"Just spit it out in the sink, Danny. Keep rinsing your mouth. I'll go downstairs and grab a cup and some salt water so you can rinse."

"No! Don't leave me. I'm scared!" Blood dripped from his mouth to his pajama tops. His red-stained lips and chin made him look like a preadolescent vampire.

"OK, I'll stay here with you, and when the bleeding stops we'll go down together." Ten minutes later the bleeding subsided, and Danny proudly handed me his tooth.

"Do you think the tooth fairy will come?" he asked excitedly.

"Yes. I'll get an envelope and you can put it under your pillow and write her a note." We went to my desk, turned on the lights and Danny composed a letter.

Dear Tooth, I hope you injoy the moller that came out of my mouth today. What I want to tell you is it was bleeding for about ten minutes but we stopp it by garguling with salt water. I hope you leave me three dollars and oh what do you do with the teeth? do you make a castle out of it? Whatever you do please leave a note of what you do with them. have a good night. Sincerely Danny.

In large letters he wrote TO TOOTH FAIRY FROM DANNY across the folded crease.

"That's a nice letter, Danny. I am sure the tooth fairy will love it. Why don't we put it under Rusty's pillow so you won't have to worry about the tooth fairy waking you up." I had already placed the tooth fairy's reply and a few dollars under the sheets of his mattress. Finally, about two in the morning I heard soft breathing. Danny was asleep. I turned out the overhead light, retrieved his letter and tooth from Rusty's bed, and left the nightlights on either side of him lit.

About four I woke up to Danny shouting, "What's that!" Rusty sat up, startled by the noise and the unfamiliar kid beside him.

"It's OK, Danny. Don't worry. You can go back to sleep."

"OK," he said in a sleepy voice. "I'm cold, Daddy..."

Without thinking, I almost told him to grab the blankets he had kicked off his bed. But in spite of being tired, I realized Danny was fragile and this was our first night together. I got out of bed and carefully avoided stepping on Rusty, Danny's backpack, the air pump he used to inflate his bed, his CD case and clothes.

It was summer solstice, and a few silver rays of moonlight shone through the slats of my partly closed wooden blinds. Danny's 75-pound body rested under a bright, clean sheet. He looked small and vulnerable.

I placed one blanket over him and noticed that a few inches of his bare toes were exposed. I overlapped another blanket and covered his feet. As I tucked him in, I spontaneously whispered, "Good night, Danny. I love you." It was the first time I said I loved him.

"I love you too, Dad," he replied half consciously. I have tucked in my nieces, nephews and other kids, but they soon go home to their own beds and families. Danny has no home—just foster parents that don't want him. As I crawled back in bed, I felt overwhelmed with feelings—emotions of feeling like a dad, sadness for the pain he endured, a fierce desire to protect Danny and an absolute awareness that every child deserves a parent to tuck them in and protect them from things that go bump in the night.

Chapter Nine

FOURTH OF JULY

At seven I woke up to Danny standing by my head. "Time to get up, Dad!"

"It's early. Don't you want to sleep a little longer?"

"Nope, let's get up..."

I turned on the TV and let him watch cartoons while I tried to sleep. Fifteen minutes later it was obvious sleep was over. Danny was thrilled with his money and letter from the tooth fairy.

Dear Danny, Thank you for your kind letter. Not many kids do that anymore—you must be special. I really appreciate your beautiful molar. As you can imagine, I need lots of teeth. What I do with them is when I fly I sprinkle the clouds so they stay beautiful and white. Sometimes children forget about me and then I don't have enough teeth to sprinkle the clouds so they turn gray. Thank you again for your note and your tooth. The Tooth Fairy

We ate breakfast and ran errands till it was time to drive Danny back to his foster home. In the car Danny asked, "Can I put my head down and pretend I'm Rusty and you tell me I'm a good dog?"

"Sure." A few minutes later Danny made a barking sound and rested his head on the console.

"Good boy," I said as I scratched his ears and patted his head. He repeated this frequently during the three-hour drive. When we were almost at his foster home he panicked.

"When can I come live with you? I don't want to go back there!" he began to cry. "Don't make me go back, Dad. I want to live with you and Rusty. I'll be good! I promise! Please! I PROMISE!"

"Danny, they're nice to you there, aren't they?"

"Sorta, but…"

"Don't worry, you can come up for a longer visit on the Fourth of July. I had a really good time with you—I love you, Danny."

"I love you too, Dad." He looked anxious. I knew he was afraid I wouldn't return.

I walked him to the front porch of his foster home, and quickly drove away. I couldn't stand watching him cry through the window again.

The next day I rested. I was exhausted from one night with him. That afternoon I called Danny's foster home to check on him. He was inconsolable and had cried all night. He kept saying he wanted his dad.

To assure Danny I was thinking of him I sent a care package every few days. When the delivery person came to the door, he told his foster parent, "She works for my dad!" The packages were a mix of books, greeting cards, trinkets and food.

Getting Danny's social worker to agree to a longer visit proved difficult. "Louise," I insisted, "I want him the whole Fourth of July weekend. We need to spend more time together."

"That's awfully rushed," she replied. "We usually recommend you have a few more one-night visits and then work your way up to a longer stay."

"I understand that, but you've already told him I'm potentially his adoptive father. Maybe if he didn't know that, it would be different. Besides, I have to drive three hours each way to pick him up. It's a lot of time in the car for one night together. You know I've asked to have Danny living with me at least a month before school begins and we need longer visits now to see how we get along."

"I think that's too fast. This is such a major transition. Maybe Danny could move in with you later in the fall—around Halloween or so."

"You want him to start fifth grade in Tacoma and then transfer schools two months later? How does that help Danny?"

Ignoring my question she asked, "What if he moves in with you the week before school starts?"

"No. He needs to get used to his new home before school starts. We can't bond if we only spend one night together every few weeks. He needs to move in soon.

Anything else is torture. Look at his fingernails. He's practically chewing them off!"

"I can't make any promises. I'll talk to my supervisor and see if she'll approve Danny spending the Fourth of July with you."

"Can you please tell her it's important? My brother is coming up from California, and I'd like Danny to meet him." Three days later, her supervisor reluctantly approved the visit.

When I arrived to pick him up, Danny jumped in my car, bounced up and down, and shouted, "Hi, Daddy! C'mon, let's get out of here!" He rummaged through the glove box, turned knobs, raised and lowered the windows and squirmed constantly. "Where's Rusty, Daddy?"

"I left him home. He likes going for drives but six hours is too long for him."

The instant we got home, Danny ran in the house shouting, "Hi, Rusty! I'm home!" He took Rusty outside while I unpacked his clothes. In the outer pocket of his backpack, Danny saved every beef jerky bag, candy wrapper and greeting card I had sent him. He brought me something too. He wrote "TO MY DAD" at least a dozen times around the outside of a box. Inside he had placed ten letters. One complimented Rusty, one raved about my mother's homemade cookies and the rest were about what a great dad I am.

On the morning of the 4th, my friend Barbara, a gifted therapist, spent a few hours with Danny. We went to her house so he could ride one of her horses. I had promised her I wouldn't let Danny move in without her meeting him. Afterward, she explained a little about his attachment issues. "Some children have a difficult time attaching to anyone. Danny is the opposite. He will attach to anyone who pays attention to him. It's the same issue, just manifested differently. If you adopt him, you're going to have your hands full."

On our way home from Barbara's house, a police car behind us turned on its lights.

"Look, Danny. There's a police officer coming. I don't think we did anything wrong, but I need to pull over."

A look of panic came over him, "Get down, Dad! Get down!" He yelled as he pulled me toward the car floor.

"Why?" I asked puzzled.

"Just get down!" I could see Danny was really upset, but I couldn't imagine why he wanted me to hide.

"Knock it off, Danny. I don't think I did anything wrong, but the officer might want to talk to us."

"But you're gay, Dad! They'll take you to jail!"

I wanted to laugh, but he was so upset that I reached over and hugged him. "Danny, police don't arrest you for being gay. I appreciate you wanting to protect me, but I don't need to hide."

"Are you sure?" he asked suspiciously.

"Yes, I'm sure. The police weren't even trying to pull us over. They were stopping the car ahead of us that was speeding."

"But I thought it was really bad to be gay, and I don't want to lose you as my dad..."

"Don't worry, Danny. The police won't arrest me and take me away because I'm gay."

The Fourth of July was hard on Danny. At my house were several boys close to his age, including my nephew. Danny didn't know anyone, and he was suspicious the other kids would steal the fireworks I got him. He didn't like it when I paid attention to other children, and he didn't act friendly toward them. I finally got him to bed around 11. At midnight he came into my room. "I'm scared, Dad."

"What's wrong, Danny?"

"All the noise!" Fireworks still interrupted the night.

"Do you want to talk?"

"No, I want to stay here with you."

"Why don't you lie on top of my bed." He snuggled near me. An explosion echoed from the beach, and Danny cringed. I put my arm around his shoulder. "It's all right, buddy."

The night before, Anacortes had the biggest thunderstorm I recall—over 3,000 lightning strikes according to the newspaper. Danny was scared, and I discovered that late at night, when he is tired, is a good time to talk.

"Danny, if you decide to come live with me and go to school here, is there a subject in school you like?"

"I like science. You break open rocks and find jewels in them."

"Have you had any problems in school?"

"No."

"Oh, because I was told you've been suspended a few times."

"Oh, yeah, I've been 'spended."

"What for?"

"Fighting. Stealing stuff."

"Do you just get mad and hit other kids?"

"Uh-huh," he sounded four years old.

"How many times do you think you've been suspended, Danny?"

He thought a moment, "About ten times."

"Are you sure?"

"Maybe 15 times… well, I'm sure it's less than 20. Can we go to bed now?"

"Sure. Good night, Danny. I love you."

"G'night, Daddy, I love you too." He hugged me and kissed my chin twice.

The next morning I saw Danny lighting firecrackers on the beach. "Danny, what are you doing!"

He avoided my glare. "Lightin' fireworks," he softly answered. The day before, we had repeated the fireworks rules many times. He knew he had to have an adult with him to light anything.

"What are the firework rules, Danny?"

"Have you or some other adult with me," he muttered.

"Is there an adult with you?"

"No..."

"You're done. That's it. No more fireworks." I grabbed them roughly out of his hand. He appeared to contemplate running, yelling or grabbing them back, but instead he walked defiantly into the house and slammed his bedroom door. I waited a few minutes and followed him. He was leaning on the foot of the queen-size bed, bawling.

"Are you all right, Danny?"

"No!" he cried through sobs.

"Are you sad about the fireworks?

"Yes! Because I can never do them again. This was my only chance, and I waited my whole life to light fireworks. Now I can't ever do them again. I HATE MY LIFE!" He started punching his stomach and moaning. I knew he believed he wouldn't light fireworks again. Danny has learned to seize opportunities when they arise or risk losing them forever.

"Danny, Danny," I murmured. "Look in my eyes." He looked up through his tears. "You will light fireworks again. I promise. I won't break my word to you. You just can't light them today. A good dad is supposed to protect his son. Fireworks are dangerous. I'm trying to have you come live with me, and if your social worker found out you were lighting fireworks alone she'd think I was a bad dad."

"You're not!" he protested. "You're the best dad in the world!"

"It's nice of you to say so—and you're a great son—but what your social worker thinks is important too. I really want to be your dad, Danny. That means I have to behave like your dad, and it helps when you try to behave like my son. It's going to be hard sometimes, but I am willing to do it if you are. The more we practice, the better we'll get at being a family. Why don't you come outside and help me take the garbage to the dump, OK?"

A smile interrupted his tears. "OK, but can we listen to my CD in the truck?" Danny never misses a chance to negotiate. Later that day he was sad when other kids lit fireworks, but he never complained. He just stared longingly at them.

My brother and I sat on the deck watching Danny and the other kids. "This is really hard," I said. "I want to let him light a few, but it feels more important to act like his dad than his buddy."

"You're right. Being a dad means you can't always be his friend. When you have to choose between being a dad and a friend, always choose being a dad. Kids can have lots of friends, but they only get one dad. You know what? I love parenting. Parenting is great—except when you actually have to parent them. Sometimes that part sucks."

Danny was inconsolable when I returned him to Tacoma. Though I did my best to soothe him, he didn't want to go back to foster care; he wanted to stay with me. A month had passed since I told the state I wanted him to move in with me, but despite many emails and phone calls, Louise hadn't given us a date.

I told my attorney how traumatized Danny was every time I returned him to foster care. She filed our petition for adoption with the court and advised me that finalizing our adoption would take six months after Danny moves in with me.

"Just keep pressing them, Jake," my attorney said. "It's a terrible system, and though I hate to say it, 'the squeaky wheel gets the grease.' They're used to adoptions taking at least a year to complete, so constantly remind them it's in Danny's best interests to live with you immediately. If they won't commit to a date, send an email to the social worker, copy her supervisor and say your attorney recommends we file a motion to ask the court to place Danny with you in his pre-adoptive home.

"You've filed your adoption petition and submitted an approved home study, so the judge would likely order Danny to be placed with you, but I doubt it will come to that. The social workers and the state's attorneys try to avoid hearings. Be persistent and keep telling them that the best thing for Danny is to move in with you immediately. If you stay focused, and remind them you're doing what's best for Danny, it will prove well in the end."

CHAPTER TEN

MOVING IN

Two days after our Fourth of July visit, Louise finally called to discuss Danny's living with me.

"When are you trying to have Danny move in with you?" Louise asked.

"In two weeks."

"That's too soon. We can't get everything ready that quickly. Besides, he needs more time to adjust to the idea of living with you."

"I don't agree. You've had over a month since I told you that I want to adopt him and have him come live with me. He doesn't need more time to adjust to leaving a foster home he hates."

"His home isn't that bad, and Danny is a hard kid to place. Not many foster parents want a kid who vandalizes, steals, lies and does poorly in school."

"You're right. Not many adoptive parents want a kid like that either. Fortunately, I do, and I want him soon. He's going crazy with anxiety—he's afraid I'll abandon him."

"Before Danny can move, we need to arrange a courtesy social worker, a meeting with his therapist, find out what resources his new school has and get an assessment of how moving will impact him. I'm sure you understand this isn't an overnight process."

"I understand you've had a month to prepare to move him. Maybe I'm not making myself clear. Either Danny comes to live with me around the end of July or I may not take him. If it will help, I'll send emails to your supervisor, Danny's CASA and the ombudsman's office saying that I told you a month ago I want to adopt Danny. I gave you an approved home study, filed a petition for adoption and said I wanted Danny placed with me soon. The waiting is killing him! Why won't you move him out of foster care? Do you want me to adopt him or not?"

"We definitely want you to adopt him, but we have to follow our procedures."

"Isn't your procedure to find permanent homes for foster kids?"

"Yes, but it isn't that…"

"If you want me to adopt him," I interrupted, "he needs to move in with me. If Danny were your son, would you leave him in foster care?"

"It isn't that simple!"

"Actually, it is. I'm either his prospective dad, or I have no relationship to him. I believe I'm Danny's best chance. I'm sorry it has come to this, but Danny needs to move in with me or I'll tell the press, the governor's office and anyone who'll listen that the state may lose his adoption because of incompetence and procrastination."

"This isn't my only case," she protested. "I can't devote all my time to it! I have other kids besides Danny I need to deal with."

"I'm sympathetic, but that isn't our problem. My focus is Danny. Look at it this way: Move Danny in with me, and you'll have one less thing to worry about."

"I'll see what I can do," she said skeptically.

"Thanks. I'll send an email reminding everyone that delaying Danny's move is harming him and if he isn't moved soon, I may not take him."

"Thanks," she replied with a hint of sarcasm.

The next day, Danny's CASA called. "I agree with your email, Jake. I'm sorry it's this difficult. The state is under a lot of pressure and doesn't work quickly. But you're right. You need to worry about Danny, and what you're demanding is the best thing for him. You're a strong advocate, and he needs that. He's out of control, and he needs this chance for a normal life."

The state didn't respond to my request to move Danny. They have learned their best defense is to ignore unwanted demands, but they didn't count on my tenaciousness.

Three days later I spoke to Ruth Davenport, Louise's supervisor.

"I'd like to know what's going on with Danny," I said.

"What do you mean?" Ruth asked.

"No one has responded to me. Is the state going to place Danny with me next week or not?"

"Oh, yes. I saw your email. This is a complex case. We need to talk to his therapist and case manager and make a determination as to how such an abrupt transition might impact him. We have to make sure that any action we take is in Danny's best interest."

I paused to make sure she was done. "He will like it."

"He'll like what?"

"He'll like moving out of a crappy foster home and coming to live with me."

"He might like it, but we need to assess if it's good for him."

"If Danny were sinking on the Titanic, would the state need a meeting to discuss the trauma he might experience if he left the ship and jumped in a lifeboat?"

"That's not a reasonable analogy."

"I think it is. Danny is sinking. He was suspended nine times last year, including the last day of school. He was kicked out of his last foster home a few months ago, and his current foster parents don't want him. Three weeks ago he ran away and had his first encounter with the police for throwing rocks at cars. I'm the only lifeboat you have, and if the state wants me, you need to treat me like his father and get him out of foster care immediately."

"Well, as Louise already told you, we aren't able to move that quickly."

"Maybe I can help you," I forced my voice to remain

calm. "I can phone my state senator and ask him to make some calls, or my attorney suggested we could file a motion asking the court to move Danny immediately. Would either of those help?"

"Who's your attorney?"

"You don't know her. She's from Seattle."

"You have a private attorney?"

"Yes. I hired my own lawyer."

"No," she replied stiffly, "we don't need your assistance. I'll take this to my area administrator and see what we can do."

"Thank you. Please keep me informed. There isn't any extra time as we only have a week."

Before I could hang up, she asked, "Why are you so focused on getting Danny moved in with you?"

"Because I'm trying to think of him as my son. If you knew my parents, you'd know that they would never leave one of their children in foster care a day longer than necessary."

I hung up the phone. *It shouldn't be this hard. Why is the state making it this difficult to bring Danny home?*

Danny's CASA and his case manager sent emails in support of Danny's moving in with me. His behavior kept deteriorating, and his foster parents said he had to leave their home soon. His case manager sent out an email that Danny's behavior was "off the wall" and he was "pushing every button and limit possible."

Louise responded by copying everyone on an email to

me saying, "We still need more time. Did you complete your background check and have your fingerprints taken? I need this prior to placing Danny with you."

Her email infuriated me. Six weeks ago I emailed Louise that my police background check and fingerprints were done. I completed them within 48 hours of receiving the forms.

I wrote a scathing reply accusing her of neglecting Danny, ignoring me and that I would sue the state for negligence if Danny wasn't moved immediately. Fortunately, I waited an hour before sending it and removed some of my references to her incompetence and the threat of a lawsuit.

Later that day my brother, a U.S. government official, called from Greece. "Hey, I read your email to the social worker you sent me."

"It looks like there's another problem. I called the state office that clears fingerprints and was told it could take up to 12 weeks to verify my identity. There is no way Danny can wait 12 weeks! He's out of control—he's doing terribly."

"If you want any help, I've worked with a lot of bureaucracies in my career. I'd be happy to look over any future letters."

"Do you think it was over the top?"

"It may have been true, but most bureaucrats don't appreciate being told how to do their jobs, and they don't usually respond well to being threatened."

"You're probably right. I was angry. Their incompetence

astounds me. I had no idea the foster-care system was this bad."

The next day, Tuesday, I had agreed to meet Danny, his therapist and his birth dad, Stan, so we could all say good-bye.

When I arrived at his therapist's office, Danny asked, "Can we go bowling?"

"That sounds a little distracting. It's a nice day. How about the zoo?" his therapist suggested. We all agreed. Danny ran, jumped and chattered constantly. He took us to the penguins, monkeys and the zoo's shark aquarium.

Whenever he said "Dad," I deferred to Stan. Danny noticed this and tried to call both of us "Dad," but it got confusing for him. Finally, at the polar bears he wanted the attention of both of us and yelled, "Dads!" Stan and I smiled at each other.

Though going to the zoo with Danny's birthfather could have been awkward, our time together felt comfortable. After an hour, the therapist pulled me aside.

"May I talk to you a moment privately?" she asked.

"Sure," I said stepping out of Stan and Danny's earshot.

"We just got a call from Danny's foster parents. They are fed up with him and won't let him return to their home. Can you take him home with you this afternoon when we're done at the zoo?"

"Right now? Today? Take him home with me permanently?"

"Yes. We have an option for emergency placements, so he can move in with you today." It shouldn't have surprised me that when it serves them the state can do what it wants, but different rules apply for children or parents. The state insists that everyone else follow their policies and rules, but they often bend or ignore them themselves.

"I can't. I am flying to Las Vegas for a trade show tomorrow so I have to stick with my plan to pick Danny up Saturday. Will he be all right till then?"

"Oh, yes, we have places we can put him for a few days. He'll go to a respite home until you can pick him up." My anxiety and efforts to bring Danny home hadn't mattered. His bad behavior produced the result he wanted—coming home with me.

After the visit, the therapist asked me to drive Danny home.

"Danny, I have some good news. You can come live with me on Saturday."

"Really? I can come live with you Saturday?"

"Yes."

"Will Rusty be there?" His eyes grew big as he bounced as high as his seatbelt allowed.

"Yes."

"For sure?"

"Yes, for sure."

"YAY!" he yelled. "WOO-HOO!" His hand shot up in the air, and he gave me a loud high-five.

"Is there something I could do to make the day you move in special?"

"Can I have a TV in my room?"

"No." I had moved the TV out of his room before his first visit.

"Can I have a computer in my room?"

"No. How about something that isn't electronic."

He thought a moment. "Could I have a banner that says 'Welcome Home, Danny'?"

"Yes, I think I can do that."

"You know that blue chair in the living room?"

"Yes…"

"Could we put it in my room? That way if I can't sleep at night I can sit in it and read."

The chair was a well-worn leather recliner. I seriously doubted his intention was to read in it, but he knew I encouraged him to read. The chair was faded from the sun, and I had considered replacing it. A few days later, I moved the old chair to his bedroom and put up a WELCOME HOME DANNY banner over his bed.

The next day, Louise called. "I wasn't able to find Danny a respite home, but I convinced his foster parents to let him stay a few more days till you pick him up on

Saturday. I wanted you to know that Danny's Aunt Lisa is trying to stop the adoption. She says she is going to hire an attorney to bring Danny home with her, but I don't think she'll do it. She doesn't have the resources, and even though Danny's sisters are with her, she doesn't have any right to Danny. His mother's rights were terminated years ago so his birthfather's wishes for adoption are what matter. She's upset we won't tell her more about you and asked me if you were gay. I said it was none of her business."

"Do I need to do anything?"

"No, you already filed the adoption petition. She's mad at the state, but this should blow over soon. I told her she could see Danny after his placement is stabilized, but until then she can't see him. She can take us to court if she wants, but she won't win."

"Do you know why she asked if I'm gay?"

"I have no idea. She just said she didn't want Danny living with a gay man. I told her whether you were gay or not is none of her business."

"Do I have to talk to her?"

"No. We'll probably approve a visit for her, but we can have an agency facilitate it so you don't have to meet her."

"Good. I don't want to meet her. Thanks for letting me know."

I hoped to have a good relationship with Danny's twin sisters, but I wasn't interested in meeting the rest of his biological family. Knowing that they couldn't take care of him and he had to live in foster care for three years was all I needed to know. Aunt Lisa's objection to Danny's adoption upset me, but staying focused on doing what was best for Danny was the right decision for both of us.

Chapter Eleven

Welcome Home Danny

On Saturday I started the drive to Tacoma to get Danny. As soon as I got in my car I felt nauseous and shaky.

I felt that I was completely inadequate to be a parent and was incapable of adopting a neglected, abused special-needs kid. My decision to have Danny live with me seemed ridiculous. I wanted to change my mind and return home alone. I've learned not to make major decisions under extreme stress or fear, so I kept driving toward his foster home, and struggled to ignore the butterflies in my stomach and sensations of panic. It felt as if I were intentionally driving off the edge of a sheer cliff. I called my mom and told her how I was feeling.

"Every parent feels that way," she said. "I was very nervous when I left the hospital with you. We had never been parents, and I couldn't believe they were sending you home with us. You're just starting a little later. You'll be fine. Danny's won the adoption lottery and doesn't even know it."

When I pulled in his driveway, Danny was playing in the front yard. He looked surprised to see me. As soon as I opened my door, he jumped up and threw his arms around my neck.

"Hi, Dad! Why are you here?"

"I'm here to take you home, Danny. I said I was coming today."

"You told me you were coming, and I tried to believe you, but my foster mom said you weren't coming till tomorrow. Why did they lie to me?" He looked ready to cry. His foster parents quickly packed his belongings in my car. He had a few cardboard moving boxes, seven black garbage bags, a bike and his skateboard.

"Did you bring Rusty?"

"No, he waited at home. It's too hot for him in the car. I told him you were coming back with me though."

Danny looked disappointed. "Ohhh, I really wanted to show him my foster home." I still felt anxious. He didn't look good either. Danny told his foster parents good-bye (I had to remind him to be polite—he couldn't wait to leave), and we drove away.

Danny sat in the front passenger seat, dwarfed by the black leather armrests and seatbacks. If he were any shorter, the law would require him to ride in the backseat. His arms were tightly crossed, and he looked grim.

"Are you happy I came to get you, Danny?"

"Yes." But he didn't look happy. He looked terrified.

"I'm glad I got to pick you up today."

"Me too," he replied. "Can you hand me your iPod?"

"Sure, it's behind my seat. Want to steer the car while I grab it," I joked.

"OK!" Danny grabbed the wheel, and the car veered sharply to the right. We narrowly missed a truck beside us.

"DANNY!" I yelled, as I shoved him away from the wheel. The truck we almost hit didn't notice us. We were both stunned.

"You hit me!" he started to cry.

"No, I didn't hit you, Danny, but I'm sorry I had to shove you. Are you OK?"

"Yeah," he said through his tears. There was a long journey ahead, and it wasn't starting out well.

"Do you remember what you asked me for to make this a special day?"

He thought a moment. "Umm... Oh, yeah. A computer?"

"No. That was what I said I wouldn't get you."

"Is it the chair for my room?" I didn't answer. "Is it? Is it? Please? Tell me! Tell me! Please?" He fluttered his eyelashes. "Just tell me and I'll be a P-L-A."

"A what?"

"A P-L-A. Perfect little angel." For a moment he pulled off a fleeting angelic countenance. Normally, he only has that if he's sleeping or very tired. I laughed.

"I can't tell you, Danny. It's a surprise. You'll see soon."

He scrunched his face, clinched his fists, glared and said, "I might be a P-L-A if you don't tell me!"

"That doesn't sound bad. I like angels."

"Sometimes it means Perfect Little 'A-s-s,'" he devilishly grinned.

When we arrived home Danny dashed out of the car and to his bedroom. Over his headboard was a banner that read WELCOME HOME DANNY. In the corner was the blue chair.

"This is so tight! I love you! Thanks, Dad!" Danny started jumping on the bed. Rusty joined him and licked Danny's legs.

"Please take your shoes off if you want to jump on the bed."

"May we take a walk? Please? I really want to go with you and Rusty to the marina. Please? It's my special night…" On Danny's Fourth of July visit we walked to the marina every evening. Danny loved watching the boats, looking in the windows of the fire station and examining the ramps kids made to jump their bikes.

When we returned home, we roasted marshmallows around a beach fire. Danny ate four s'mores (one uncooked) and played with Charlotte, my friend's ten-year-old daughter.

The next morning I woke up at six. The previous day seemed surreal. I crept down the hall to Danny's room. He was there, still asleep. I tried to go back to bed but couldn't. I picked up *Parenting with Love and Logic* and *Adopting the Hurt Child* and paged through them. I had read many books about parenting, attachment disorders, ADHD and adopting older, special-needs children. Though I discovered some great books, relying on them to become a good parent felt as useless as reading in fourth grade about how to be a good football player. I never learned to be athletic reading a book.

Later that day we took a drive. "So this is where I'll go to school, Dad?" Danny asked as we passed the local elementary school. He calls me Dad constantly.

"Yep, that's your school."

"Oh…"

"You had some problems at your last school didn't you, Danny?"

"Yeah, I got suspended."

"Is there anything I can do to help you succeed in your new school?"

"Can I have a therapist?"

"Yes, you'll have a therapist," I said. His first appointment was in a few days. "Can you think of anything else?"

"Yeah. When I get mad, I need a three-minute time-out to breathe and calm down. Do you think I can get that?" he looked worried.

"I don't know, Danny, but it sounds like a good idea to me. We can talk to your teacher about it."

A few hours later, we got home and Danny went next door to play with Charlotte. "Do you mind if we take him to the waterslide park for a few hours?" her dad, Ken, asked. I liked the idea of his going, but I was uncertain about his behavior. My 17-year-old nephew offered to go with them and help watch Danny, so I agreed.

After they left, I took a brief nap and returned some phone calls. Though Danny had been there only a day, I enjoyed having a short break from him, but I worried about his behavior at the waterslides. I called Ken.

"How's it going?"

"They're having a great time. Your nephew is tuckered out, but Danny and Charlotte are going strong."

"Have you had any problems?"

Ken laughed. "No, he's just real active. He'll fit right in with the other boys at his school." I hoped so. Danny's last school was described to me as one of the worst in the state. The social worker called it a "pre-gang" elementary school, and Danny was hanging out with the wrong kids. The schools in our neighborhood don't have many gangs, but they do have country kids who know how to milk a cow, raise pigs, ride a tractor and throw a punch.

When Danny returned home, he played on the beach. Occasionally he dashed by the front deck where I relaxed. Sometimes he'd stop and ask if he could have a Popsicle, a glass of water, ride his bike to the marina or make a jump ramp. Other than Danny's constantly interrupting me, it felt like most evenings at the beach with friends—relaxing, peaceful and memorable.

Danny's state psychiatrist had increased his ADHD medication from 20 milligrams to 30 milligrams earlier that week. Danny got a terrible headache within an hour of taking his higher dose. I went back to his original dosage. I found it incredible his psychiatrist was trying to manage Danny's behavior by increasing his medication. The reason he was anxious, nervous, excited and acting out was obvious—he was about to join a new family.

During Danny's first two weeks with me, I tried to spend most of each day with him. This meant I didn't go to work or he came with me. I did some of both. On a previous visit, I asked Danny if he could swim and he assured me he was a fine swimmer. When I asked to see him swim, he explained he didn't actually swim but he didn't need to wear a lifejacket because he always floats.

"Danny, when you are in the ocean you have to wear a life jacket, and if you want to try paddling the kayaks you need to take swimming lessons."

"I don't want to take swimming lessons! I don't need to know how to swim, and I don't want to use those stupid kayaks," he protested. "They make my butt wet!"

"Danny, I won't make you go in the water, but every morning you're going to be in a swimsuit at the YMCA pool. You can decide if you get in, but that's where you're going to be."

"I don't wanna go. Besides, my swimsuit gives me wedgies and it isn't comfy. Hmmph!" He glared at me with his arms crossed. As we drove to the YMCA, he kept protesting. "I'm NOT going in the water, you know."

"I know."

"So why are we going then? I'm not going in! I don't need to swim." I didn't reply. "You know I'm not going in, right? Right? RIGHT!"

"We're going to the pool," I replied calmly. "You can tell your instructor you're not going in. If you're too scared, you don't have to go in the water. Maybe she can teach you to swim while you sit on the bleachers watching the other kids in the pool."

When we arrived Danny said he had to go to the bathroom. He took long enough to make us late. At the pool, his cute, young, female instructor had Danny in the water, jumping, diving, splashing and laughing within two minutes.

On the way out, Danny said, "That was fun! Are we going tomorrow? Did you see me jump? I jumped in nine feet of water!" Danny has never had a parent take him to swim lessons, attend school recitals or cheer him on at his baseball games.

"You did a great job jumping in, Danny! You're going to be an awesome swimmer. We can go back tomorrow and the rest of the week."

"Hurray! I love swimming, Dad."

When we got to my warehouse, I reminded Danny he had to work.

"Danny, you know that Chuck is your boss here, right?"

"I thought you were the boss."

"No, Chuck is the boss, and you need to keep him happy. Otherwise I can't bring you to work."

"But isn't this your company?" he persisted.

"Yes, it's my company but it's part Chuck's too, and since I'm your dad I don't want to be your boss."

"Ohhh, OK," he sighed.

Chuck showed him how to fill out a time card. A few minutes later, Danny came running into the office shouting, "Hi, Rusty!" Rusty ran to him, eager to enjoy the new excitement at work. Our office manager, Carolyn, was on the phone and Danny's yelling made it impossible for her to concentrate.

"C'mon, Rusty! Want a treat? Jump up! Jump up!" Danny held a treat as Rusty leaped to grab it from his hand.

"Danny," Carolyn said. He didn't respond. "Danny," she said, louder.

"Uh-huh," he replied still playing with Rusty.

"When you come into the office, you can't yell. You need to speak in a normal voice and make sure I'm off the phone before you talk to me, OK?"

"Uh-huh," he said as he ran back into the warehouse. Ten minutes later he came back in the office. He crossed the threshold slowly and in a mock whisper said, "See, Carolyn? Look at how quiet I am!" Danny wants to behave, but because of his lack of impulse control he often lands in trouble.

Danny made a workspace for himself in the warehouse. During his breaks, he gathered old phones, a credit-card reader and a small gumball machine to set up his office.

The rest of the week was filled with minor injuries, whining about bedtime, swim lessons, bike riding, playing with Rusty, sassing me, singing off key in the car and transforming clean clothes to dirty ones in 15 minutes.

When we went to the mall to eat at the food court and buy clothes that fit (Danny shops quickly—we had socks, underwear, shoes, shirts and jeans in under an hour), he licked his plate like a dog and poured huge amounts of ketchup and salt on his food. I praised him frequently for his positive behaviors and tried to ignore all but the worst ones. No matter where we were, he constantly called me Dad.

When we sorted through his belongings from foster care, almost everything was garbage. He owned a broken stereo, damaged toys, clothes too tight, eight pair of shoes too small, five Bibles, a math textbook he stole (he claimed it was to get better at arithmetic), and one photo album with 15 pictures. He also had more than 100 youth-size diapers.

"Why do you have all these diapers, Danny?"

"So I don't get the bed wet."

"Do you wear them every night?"

"Uh-huh."

"Do they work?"

"Not really. They just make me wet the bed more. I hate them! I'm too old for them, and I'm not going to wear them anymore!"

"Good. I don't think you should wear them anymore either."

"Really?" his eyes lit up.

"Really. It's not that big a deal. Here's what we're going to do. Take all those diapers and shove them in the garbage can. You're ten and you're too old to wear them. I'll put a waterproof pad on your mattress. If you wet the bed, we'll change the sheets together and take care of it, OK?"

"Yay! Yay!" He crammed the diapers into the garbage can. "This is fun, Dad!"

When we laid everything he owned on the garage floor, it didn't seem much for ten years of life. Other than the diapers, Danny didn't want to throw anything away. But when I explained we could donate the clothes and shoes that didn't fit to needy kids, he was happy to be rid of them. We saved a few things that had special meaning to him—I didn't want him to lose anything of sentimental value.

Kids in foster care move regularly. Their belongings are packed in garbage bags or cardboard boxes. Their clothes often arrive dirty, and their belongings aren't so much packed as dumped. It is usually the goal of their caregiver to ensure that every sign of the kid leaves when the child moves. It's sadly ironic that most foster kids find everything they own packed in garbage bags, as they are shuffled from one temporary home to another like society's cast-offs.

Danny's personal stigma is so deeply ingrained he isn't aware of how differently he perceives himself from other kids. I see it in his words and actions. Families are something he has learned about more from movies and TV than from personal experience. His perceptions bear no more relationship to reality than when I watched Disney's *Jungle Book* and asked my parents to send me to India so I could become like Mowgli.

Danny will likely be all right. He has an extraordinary support system now and a strong advocate in me. But what about the other seven-, eight-, and nine-year-olds languishing in homes where no one reads them a story or tucks them in bed at night? Then there are the teenagers; hardly anyone wants them.

The key to helping the many is helping the one. I see how to help only Danny. Yet, when I witness his desperation for a family and his need to be noticed, loved and embraced, I can't help thinking of the millions of children in the world like him. What is going to happen to them?

CHAPTER TWELVE

WEEK ONE

Every night of our first week together, I spent half an hour lying on Danny's bed talking about our day, reading him stories and helping him fall asleep. He loves *The Three Billy Goats Gruff* and *The Boxcar Children*. As I read to him, snuggled and listened to more of his life story, my affection toward him grew.

Last night Danny told me about watching Uncle Robby hit "Grandpa" Eddie (his grandmother's physically abusive, alcoholic boyfriend) on the head with a baseball bat. The police and paramedics responded. Danny witnessed it all.

"You could see part of Grandpa Eddie's bones," he whispered. "But I'm glad he got hit."

"Why, Danny? Did Eddie hit you?"

"Sometimes. Once he tried to kidnap my grandma and we had to hide so he couldn't hurt us. The police came and he went to jail. But the worst thing was when he killed my rabbit. I was only five!" he started to cry.

"What happened?"

"I built a rabbit jungle in my closet. I even made a litter box. I didn't know what to call my bunny so my sister said I could name it 'Rabbit.' That's a good name, isn't it, Dad?"

"I think that's a great name. It was the name of the rabbit in Winnie-the-Pooh. What color was Rabbit?"

"She was gray. She loved rabbit jungle. Both my sisters had rabbits, and they played in rabbit jungle too. When Grandpa Eddie saw rabbit jungle, he got really mad and started yelling and cussing at me. He grabbed Rabbit and took her downstairs. I snuck after them and followed them outside. He took Rabbit to the garage and came out holding a knife with blood on it."

"Did he say he killed Rabbit?"

"No. He said he didn't know what happened to her. But I saw the knife and I never saw Rabbit again. What I want to know is why did he kill her? He didn't kill my sisters' rabbits. Why do bad things always happen to me?" Danny cried as I held him and stroked his bristly crew-cut hair.

"I don't know, Danny. Sometimes life isn't fair. It's sad, isn't it? I'm sorry about Rabbit." When he stopped crying, I said, "It's time to go to sleep now. I hope you have good dreams. Do you know what I hope you dream about?"

"My rabbit?"

"Yes, your rabbit. I love you."

"I love you too, Dad." He hugged me, kissed me twice and fell asleep.

We have been together a week, and I have no regrets

about trying to become Danny's dad other than my loss of sleep, constant interruptions and needing to consider his needs instead of only my own.

When I took the garbage out this morning, there was my scooter lying in the yard, red lava rocks in the driveway, the garbage can overflowing and an empty root-beer bottle standing forlornly in the grass.

So this is parenting, I thought.

The next morning I woke to see Danny standing in front of my nightstand. "Dad! Dad! I had a really bad nightmare, and I wet the bed!" Danny held his urine-soaked clothes while draped in a towel. It was six a.m.

"Are you all right, Danny?"

"Yeah, I'm fine. See, I didn't hide my clothes!" In foster care embarrassment, punishment and being forced to wear diapers led Danny to hiding his underwear and pajamas when he wet the bed. To try to stop him from hiding his clothes, his caregivers rewarded him with "Evergreen bucks," a fiat-money foster-care currency he could use to buy toys, go to a movie or get candy whenever he turned in urine-soaked bedclothes.

The plan accomplished two things: Danny always turned in his wet clothes, and he began peeing in them more frequently. He quickly realized he could earn money.

Surprisingly to me, there have been times when I am glad Danny is in pain "for his own good." Yesterday he had a tantrum and tried to kick me. Earlier in the week he scraped his knee and used the scab as an excuse to move slowly, avoid chores and seek attention. As his legs thrashed in an effort to strike me, I grabbed his injured knee. He screamed as if I'd lit his finger on fire.

"You hurt my knee... you hurt me... Oh! Oh! ARGGH!"

"Sometimes when you kick people, things like that happen. You need to go to your room and calm down."

"I DON'T WANT TO!"

"I know, but you have to, so get going."

"I HATE YOU!"

"That's OK. I love you. Do you want to sing your anger song?"

"No! I hate that!" He slammed his bedroom door. One of my books about special-needs kids suggested having a child sing an anger song when she or he is upset. When I proposed it to Danny, we both laughed. He didn't think it was funny now.

I didn't imagine how physically and emotionally draining parenting could feel, nor did I imagine the glow in my heart when Danny's arms are wrapped around my neck and he whispers, "I love you, Dad."

Danny graduated from swimming class and started attending a local Christian day camp. He came home singing about Jesus and telling me how much he loved his counselors. The camp director has multiple sclerosis and uses a motorized wheelchair on the hard-packed forest paths. He pulled me aside when I dropped Danny off.

"We love having Danny here. He's exactly the kind of kid we want to help. We don't get enough like him. I've watched him closely, and he is beaming. I don't think he's done too much beaming. Thanks for giving us a chance to be part of his life."

I was apprehensive about enrolling Danny in a Christian camp, but I am glad I did. His street swagger and attitude are fading. Like many foster kids, he has learned to adapt to new surroundings like a chameleon and could resurrect his old behaviors quickly. Fortunately, he enjoys his new identity.

At bedtime tonight Danny asked, "Dad, what's a GTA?"

"I don't know. Where did you hear that?"

"My camp counselor. He graduated from high school and needed a GTA to go to college."

"I think he meant GPA. It means grade point average."

"How do I get one?"

"When you go to middle school, you'll get it on your report card. It's a way of keeping track of your grades."

"Ohhh…"

"Do you want to go to college?"

"Yeah, I do."

"That may be hard since you don't do homework." Danny has never done homework and told me that even if he wants to he will never be able to do it.

He thought a moment. "I might be able to do homework if you gave me candy," he hinted.

"Do you want to go to college?"

"Yes."

"Why?"

"It's the good path."

"What's the good path?"

"A clean house, pets like Rusty and a loving dad like you!" He jumped on the bed and grabbed my neck to break his fall as he landed.

"OW! That hurts!"

"Sorry, Daddy!" He looked concerned.

"It's OK. Just watch my neck. What's the bad path?"

"Jail, drugs, gangs, alcohol, like in Tacoma."

"That doesn't sound good. Why do you want the good path?"

"To be happy and so I can be with you!" He grabbed my neck again, but this time gently.

"That sounds great, Danny. Good night."

"Dad?"

"Yes…" I wanted to leave his bedroom. Rusty was curled on the floor trying to sleep, and I needed time to myself. "What, Danny?"

"I really want you to adopt me." I had told him several times we need to get to know each other to decide if we want to create a family. It won't work if we don't both want to do it.

"I want you to be my son, Danny but it's going to take time. Try not to worry, OK?"

"I'll try," he said dubiously, "but I'm going to worry because I always want you to be my dad."

"Thanks, Danny. I want to be your dad. I leaned down and gave him one last kiss. "You're my favorite boy in the world. I love you. Good night."

CHAPTER THIRTEEN

BOO!

A few weeks after Danny moved in, my friend Leslie invited me for dinner. I knew she was concerned about how I was doing as a single parent. "Are you OK, Jake?" she asked. "You look so tired and stressed."

"I am, but it's getting better. Have you noticed how much Danny has changed?" My voice brightened as I talked about him.

"He's like a different person. He doesn't look the same as the boy you introduced me to a few months ago. He not only acts differently, he looks different."

"I know. I look about five years older, my eyes are puffy, my hip hurts from sleeping wrong and I think a lot of my healthy, happy energy has gone to Danny, but that's OK. He needs it more than I do."

Danny is thriving. He gained 13 pounds in six weeks, he is eager to please, and he tries to follow my directions. He's enjoying being a kid and having an attentive dad.

But I miss my old life. The lack of sleep, incessant chatter, shifting of priorities and loss of balance and serenity is a shock to my body, mind and soul. I feel like I've jumped naked into a cold swimming pool and I won't ever adjust to the temperature.

Fortunately, I am more convinced than ever that being Danny's dad is the right decision for me. As arduous as it feels, I don't question what I am doing. I have a new respect, appreciation and empathy for parents—especially my own.

Three weeks after Danny moved in, I had a meeting in Los Angeles. I brought Danny along so I could surprise him by taking him to Disneyland. He had never left Washington State or been on an airplane before. The thought of flying terrified him.

Danny had watched the movie *Castaway*, in which Tom Hanks survives a plane crash. He kept asking me how to tell if the plane was crashing, if we would survive and what would happen if I died and he lived. As the plane took off, he got excited. He loved the feeling of acceleration. Other than some small moments of panic from air turbulence, he did fine.

When we arrived in Los Angeles, I drove directly to Disneyland. As we walked toward the entrance, Danny kept trying to figure out where we were. Finally, he blurted out, "Are we in Disneyland, Dad?" The tourists wearing Mickey Mouse ears were a dead giveaway.

I didn't answer. "Danny, I wrote you a letter. I want you to sit down and read it."

Dear Danny,

Since you have been living with me, I haven't written you as often as when you were in foster care.

I am very proud of you. It is hard to become part of a new family, and every day I appreciate how hard you are trying to become a good son. It makes me proud to be your father.

The first time we met, you said the only place in the world you wanted to go was Disneyland. I didn't know then if I would be able to adopt you, so I didn't tell you that Disneyland is one of my favorite places too.

Today is the day, Danny. We are going to Disneyland together. I believe the reason Disneyland is called the happiest place on earth is because it is a place to share and play in with the people you love most. I love you. I am proud of you, you are a GREAT son, and I can't wait to go to Disneyland with you. Love, Dad

When he finished reading the letter he looked up puzzled. "Really? We're at Disneyland? Right now?"

"Yes, Danny." He was in disbelief. He had experienced too many broken promises to trust me.

"Can we go on some rides?" It wasn't an idle question. He needed me to prove we were really here.

"Yes. We can go right now."

"Really?"

"Really."

"Hurray! Hurray! I'm in Disneyland and I am going

on rides! C'mon, Dad! C'mon!" Danny jumped up and pulled my arm toward the entrance. He chose to ride the Haunted Mansion first. He enjoyed it so much he didn't want to leave, but after the third time through I made him try riding the Pirates of the Caribbean.

Our day in Disneyland passed quickly. Danny was well behaved, enthusiastic and excited for most of it.

When we got to our hotel room, I went to the bathroom to brush my teeth. I noticed from the slight odor that Danny had just used the toilet. As I reached for the toothpaste, I saw that the toilet paper was still folded in a triangular point that hotel maids leave at the end of the roll.

"Hey, Danny."

"What."

"Did you just go to the bathroom?"

"Uh-huh," he replied. All his attention was on the cartoons on TV.

"Did you wipe?"

"Uh-huh," he said, still not paying attention to me.

"Danny!" He jerked his head toward me. "Please show me what toilet paper you used in the bathroom."

He glared at me—angry that I interrupted the cartoon and resentful I was prying into his personal hygiene. "Fine! I didn't wipe!"

"I didn't think so. You need to come back to the bathroom and wipe now, and don't flush the toilet. I want to see the toilet paper." He didn't move. "NOW, DANNY!"

"Uggh," he groaned then muttered something.

"What was that?" I asked.

"Nuthin…" He went in the bathroom for 30 seconds and hurried back to watch cartoons.

"Are you done?" The paper evidence in the toilet bowl wasn't compelling.

"Yes."

"Is your bottom clean?"

"I don't know. How would I know?"

"What do you mean you don't know?"

"I don't want to look at it!" He scrunched his face in disgust. "That's nasty!"

"Actually, you do need to look at the toilet paper and wipe until the poop is gone."

"But that will take forever!" he groaned. I just stared at him. "Fine!" He moved his arms in exasperation and returned to the bathroom.

"How often do you use toilet paper, Danny? Tell the truth. I am looking in your eyes." I've taught him that eyes are the windows to the soul and by looking in his eyes I can see if he is telling the truth. I am teaching him to do the same with me.

He shrugged. "'Bout once or twice a week. I don't need no toilet paper!" I groaned inwardly. One advantage I assumed I had with a ten-year-old was solid toileting habits.

"Danny, you need to use toilet paper every time. Not just a few times a week."

He scrunched his face in disgust. "I got better things to do than sit around and wipe my butt!"

When we returned home, my brother, his wife and four kids had arrived from Greece for three weeks. My sister, her husband and four kids were staying at my parents' house, and my other brother, his wife and son moved into the apartment behind my house for a few days. It was my mom and dad's 50th wedding anniversary, and they invited and paid for all their kids and grandkids to join them on a seven-day cruise to Alaska.

Danny played with my nine nieces and nephews for the week leading up to my parent's anniversary. On the day of the reception, Danny grew increasingly anxious about going. I had purchased a card for all the grandkids to sign and I passed it to Danny. Instead of signing his name he wrote, "BOO!" in large letters. I was furious with him.

"Why did you write 'BOO!,' Danny? I tried to keep my voice calm.

"I mean BOO!" he chanted as he made big thumbs-down motions with his hand. "BOO!" I glared at him.

"GET IN YOUR ROOM NOW! I am really upset with you! You ruined my card, we're late, and you aren't even dressed yet. GET GOING NOW!"

"I'm not getting dressed, and I'm not going!" he shouted. Without thinking, I grabbed him by the back of his neck and shoved him toward his bedroom. When we walked in, I pushed him roughly onto his bed.

"YOU'RE HURTING ME!" he yelled.

"Good! But don't worry, Danny," my voice changed to an icy, measured tone, "I won't be hurting you anymore. You're right. You're not going. You're not going on the cruise either. I'm going to miss my parent's 50th wedding anniversary and stay home to babysit you. Do you know where you are going? You're going back to foster care for a week while I go on a cruise and think about whether I even want to adopt a kid like you!"

As the words escaped, my initial rage slowly dissipated. I knew I had gone too far. At the same time, a sadistic, cold, oppressive part of me, repressed and caged for years, exulted at finally being free. This malevolent part of my being enjoyed physically dominating Danny and thrived on his terror that he might have to return to foster care.

"Dad! Dad! Please don't leave me, I love you. Please. Please! Please! I love you, Daddy! Please don't leave me! You're the only dad I have, and I waited five years to get adopted. Please don't leave me!"

Tears flew everywhere. His face contorted in agony as he continued to plead through his weeping and his runny nose. "You're the best daddy in the world. No one ever loved me like you do, not my Aunt Lisa, not anyone. Please don't make me go back, Dad. Please! I HATE MYSELF!!!"

He started hitting himself hard in the stomach and face as he wailed inconsolably. I didn't feel a thing. Instead, I enjoyed watching the young child in front of me experience sheer terror.

"You don't care about me, Danny. You don't care

about my family, and you ruined my mom and dad's 50th anniversary card. I don't know what I am going to do."

"I can fix the card, Daddy. Please don't send me away! Please!" He gripped his arms tightly around my neck, and his tears smeared across my face. He looked directly in my eyes and said, "I love you, Dad. Please don't ever leave me. WHEN YOU DIE I WANT THEM TO KILL ME AND PUT ME IN YOUR CASKET SO WE CAN ALWAYS BE TOGETHER!" His tears covered my cheek and neck, but I didn't hug him back. I gave him no affection.

Despite everything I knew about Danny's background of neglect, abandonment and abuse, I didn't choose love. I chose to feed my icy rage with his pain. I was enjoying his suffering.

Then, I had a moment of clarity. Some higher part of my being slapped me into consciousness. I knew we were at a crossroads, that this moment was supremely important—it felt as if it had been for lifetimes—and how I acted, right now, would affect both of us for the rest of our lives. I did the only thing I've learned to do when I know I am wrong and lost. I prayed with all the intensity I could summon, *God, help me! PLEASE, GOD, HELP ME!*

Immediately I felt a wave of calm and grace envelop, encircle and protect my body. My skin tingled and my spirit became alert. The ice surrounding my soul cracked open, and I felt like the Grinch realizing his heart for the first time on Christmas morning. In that moment I knew I passed this test.

I grabbed Danny in my arms and cradled him. "I love you, Danny. If you want me to adopt you, I'm going to adopt you... I went crazy. I'm so sorry, buddy. You didn't deserve that. I lost my temper... I am so, so sorry." I kept stroking his head and rocking him side to side.

"Please don't leave me," he said through his quiet sobs. "Just don't leave me, Daddy. I need you. You're the only dad I have," he ran his little fingers tenderly through my hair.

"I won't leave you, Danny. I won't leave you." I held him as if he were four years old and his kitten had just died. We stayed like that a long time. Finally I said, "Danny, we need to go to grandpa and grandma's anniversary party. Do you think you can go?" He nodded, put on his clothes, and we started to leave.

"Wait, Dad. Wait!"

"What is it, Danny?"

"I have to fix Grandma's card!" He changed "BOO!" to "I can't wait to get on the BOAT!"

Two of Danny's best qualities are that he is clever at creating solutions and that he doesn't hold grudges. Within an hour he was playing with other kids at the party, having fun and behaving well.

My parents enjoyed a wonderful reception, and I got to see many relatives and friends, but I was haunted by my behavior. Why did I enjoy seeing my new son in pain? *There is more to parenting than meets the eye,* I thought.

Chapter Fourteen

New School

Danny loved the family cruise to Alaska. He caught his first salmon in Ketchikan, rode a dogsled in Skagway and enjoyed spending time with his new relatives. He particularly attached to his older cousins. He received lots of love from my family; they treated him as one of them.

Shortly after the cruise, Louise drove from Tacoma to visit Danny. State law requires Danny's social worker to visit him at least once a month.

"I hate this new law," she complained.

"What law is that, Louise?"

"We have to come in person to see each kid once a month. It's really hard when they live so far away like you and Danny."

I nodded sympathetically, but inside I was seething. Louise is attractive and comes off well in court, but she drags her feet and doesn't follow up unless harassed.

"Danny seems to be doing great," she said. "I can't believe how well he behaved on that cruise. Stealing is such a problem for him that I was sure people would be missing things. When I asked Danny why he didn't steal anything on the trip, he said now that he lives with you he has everything he needs so he doesn't steal anymore." She seemed confused by Danny's explanation.

"He's doing really well," I agreed, changing the subject. "Do you know when you can transfer Danny's file to the adoption social worker?" Louise was supposed to transfer the file over a month ago. His adoption would be stuck until she got it done. Louise sighed.

"The thing is Jake, I hate to say this…but you guys are doing great, so I need to neglect your case."

"Why would you neglect our case because we're doing great?"

"My supervisor told me I need to prioritize my time on my cases in crisis, and since you guys are doing fantastic I can't work on your case."

If you want a crisis, I can give you one, I thought. With a fixed smile, I replied, "I appreciate everything you're doing, but you know the adoption can't move forward until you transfer the file to the adoption social worker."

"I'll get to it as soon as I can," Louise answered sympathetically.

The level of incompetence, apathy and bureaucracy surrounding Danny boggles me. It took ten phone calls and three trips to different social service offices to have his medical insurance updated to a different plan. I spend at least 25% of each day dealing with bureaucratic issues, and it is wearing me down.

The irony is that the State of Washington budgets tens of thousands of dollars annually toward each foster kid, and because Danny is labeled a level four (the most difficult kids in the state system), the state spends more than average on him. Despite that, when Danny moved in most of his clothes didn't fit, he ate poorly, he barely read at a second-grade level, he was forced to take psychotropic medication, and he was usually anxious, impulsive or scared. Though it is in Danny's and the state's interests to complete his adoption quickly, each week brings new bureaucratic hurdles and unnecessary delays.

Fortunately, my experience with Danny's new school was better than my interaction with the child-welfare agency. Before the first day of school, I met with Danny's new teacher and principal and shared some of his background. We created a plan to help him start the year successfully.

His teacher, Sarah, had taught for decades and understood at-risk kids. The principal was new to the school, but she had spent the past few years working with special-needs elementary-age students. They seemed like the perfect team for Danny. I volunteered to tutor in his classroom every other Tuesday so I could get a better sense of his challenges.

Danny's progress the first month of school was remarkable. He turned in homework, behaved fairly well in class and tried to make friends. Recently he had two classmates over for dinner. It was the first time in his life he felt comfortable having friends over to his house after school. Listening to him laugh, yell, play and show off his bedroom gave me chills of joy.

Danny is beginning to feel like my son, and many of the challenges we face seem typical. When I drove home from work a few days ago, I found the driveway obstructed because he had left cinder blocks in an attempt to build a bike jump ramp. When I walked in the house, I was annoyed that he didn't run up and greet me with a hug (he always has before, but today he ignored me). Instead, he handed me a note from his teacher that two homework assignments were missing.

"Don't worry, Dad. That note from my teacher you need to sign isn't important," he lied. "I don't have to make up the homework. She just sent the note home because the school makes her do it." After I questioned him, he admitted he was lying. An hour later I was still angry, but I realized I was upset by typical-ten-year-old behavior. This was success!

At Danny's therapy appointment, his counselor asked us what challenges we need to work on. "Danny is telling a lot of impulsive lies. Usually not too important ones—just spur-of-the-moment annoying lies," I answered.

"I don't know why, but I keep doing it," he interjected. "I stopped for a little bit, but now it's starting again! Last night when my dad's friend took me to the high school game, I lied and told her I went to an Eminem concert. Then I told some kids I rode a horse to the mall and they all laughed at me." He hung his head.

The therapist looked closely at me. "Is that all? Impulsive lying?"

I looked at Danny. He nodded. "Yes, I think that's it."

"That's great. We can work on the lying, but overall you guys are doing great."

It is great. Danny hasn't bitten or hit me in weeks (he bit my arm hard three times the first month he lived with me), his hygiene has improved dramatically, he wets the bed rarely (not more than once every few weeks), and he has been off all psychotropic drugs for six weeks. I stopped giving him the medication so a new psychologist could evaluate him. His behavior didn't noticeably deteriorate, and his appetite and sleeping patterns improved, so with the conditional approval of his psychiatrist, he is off all meds.

Last night Danny asked me if I would still adopt him if he gets suspended from school. "Why would you be suspended, Danny? You're doing fine."

"I hit a kid, Dad. He makes me so mad! I just wanted to see his blood!" His eyes looked violent as he started popping his knuckles.

"Why did you hit him?"

"He kicked me on purpose in soccer! He says I can't play soccer, and I can, so when he kicked me I punched him."

"Did you tell him you were sorry?"

"No! And today I hit him again at recess, so tomorrow I'll 'probly be suspended..." He looked upset and his grammar reverted to a five-year-old's.

I was angry. I hate bullies. "Danny, you can't hit him! Tomorrow you need to tell him you're sorry. Do you have any idea of how you can stop hitting him?"

"No. I just want to see his blood. I don't think I can stop."

"That's not acceptable! You need to come up with a solution."

"Maybe I could transfer to the other fifth-grade class. I like my teacher, but every time I see that kid he makes me mad, and if I were in the other class I wouldn't have to see him."

"No, that's not a solution. You have to learn to get along with people you don't like. You're staying in your classroom."

"Ohhh," he whined.

That night I wrote an email to Danny's teacher about my concern for the other kid's safety. I also mentioned that I was having Danny tested for ADHD and learning disabilities and I hoped to leave him off medication. The next morning she replied.

Jake, I have talked privately with the other child, and he said there was no problem with Danny. None of the supervisors turned in anything about hitting. It is my guess that Danny is testing to see what your response would be to him getting in trouble. You are right to encourage him to practice his self-control and learning to get along with others. Perhaps reassuring him that you aren't giving up on him just because he makes mistakes along the way is what he is searching for. We all fall short of being perfect, but we get up, right the wrongs, and try again.

About the medication, I am fine to wait until you finish Danny's big evaluation. He is fidgety but certainly NOT bouncing off the walls in an uncontrolled way (I have had those kids too). I hope this helps. Let me know if anything more comes up. Sarah

As I read her response, I realized she was right. Danny was testing me. Sarah is passionate, gifted, experienced and kind. She makes all teachers look good, and I valued her opinion.

Could Danny really not need medication? He had been drugged for at least four years, and all his caregivers were warned not to take him off medication for even a day. Yet with two months drug-free, Danny is doing better emotionally, behaviorally and scholastically than he ever has before.

I wondered how much of Danny's progress was from living in a loving, stable environment, having frequent nurturing contact with me, thriving in a small classroom with a phenomenal teacher, being off medication, having a good therapist, or his willingness to make the most of the opportunity he had. It seems to me that everything came together and he is doing far better than I had imagined. I give most of the credit to him. No matter how good his environment, if Danny didn't have the desire to grow and change, none of his new opportunities would matter. He would still be languishing in the hopeless state he was in— only his environment would have improved.

My first parenting goal for Danny was to help him grow up without ending up in prison. His social workers described him as one of many "thrownaway" foster kids they work with who appear destined to bounce from foster home to foster home, get involved with the juvenile justice system, abuse drugs, drop out of school and likely end up homeless or institutionalized. But watching the miracle of his transformation makes me hope for more. I believe that Danny, like all children, is a unique and special being with gifts and potential beyond my ability to see.

There are still problems. Sometimes when I wake up and lay in bed thinking about the day, I resent having to make him breakfast, shuttle him back and forth to school, feed him dinner, make sure his homework is done and get him to bed. My weekends are filled with corn mazes, magic shows, movies, dirty laundry, wet clothes from hiking in the creek, constant requests for sugar, kid TV shows, top-20 music, incessant noise and nonstop motion.

I miss quiet moments to read, the sound of my grandmother's clock ticking in my silent, serene living room, having responsibility for no one's needs but my own, and time to indulge in food, books, shopping, movies for grown-ups, long phone calls and watching what I want on television.

The things I miss aren't that important—they're just activities I've grown accustomed to. Most of the time it's all right, but when I feel tired, annoyed, insecure or angry, it's hard to avoid making Danny the target of my resentments.

When I'm feeling overwhelmed, it helps to remember that Danny didn't start our relationship by asking me to be his dad—I approached him to be my son. Both of us brought our own hopes and dreams to the idea of creating a family together.

It's far too easy to forget that as much as I dreamed of having a child, Danny dreamed of having a loving dad. Creating a family isn't just about me getting a child or becoming a father. It's also about Danny getting a dad and becoming a son. The grace is found in the reciprocity between us. The miracle is in how well it is working.

CHAPTER FIFTEEN

PARENTS AND BIRTH FAMILY

One of the unexpected consequences of becoming Danny's dad is meeting his friend's parents. Although I know many children, I have met most of them through their moms or dads. Now I am meeting kids through Danny, and as inevitably as meeting a salesman's boss when buying a car, I am forced to interact with their parents.

Some of them are benign, pleasant and responsible. Others don't work and wear ragged Budweiser T-shirts. His friend's dad, Mark, is going through a bitter divorce and likes to drink alcohol. The first time I was at Mark's house, I dropped off his son after cross-country practice. Mark invited me in, offered me a beer, and proceeded to tell me the status of his divorce.

"Teresa is such a bitch! She thinks I am going to move out of this house for her? She's got another thing coming. I told her I'd leave next summer, but I'm not going anywhere," his eyes flashed in anger as he rapidly clenched his fists. "You sure you don't want a beer, bro?"

"Uh, no. Thanks anyway, Mark. You might as well know I am in recovery and haven't had a drink in over 20 years."

"Good for you, bro! You can be my designated driver. All this parenting stuff must be new for you. Do you ever need a break from Danny?

Thinking he was offering to occasionally watch Danny I replied, "I don't get out much but I do need a break sometimes."

"Great! Why don't we go out drinking and you can be the driver?" I politely declined. Earlier this week I took Danny to Mark's house to drop off some schoolwork. I had been there five minutes when his soon-to-be ex-wife, Teresa, arrived. We greeted each other politely, and she asked if I could help her unload two beanbag chairs from her car.

"Sure. Where are we putting them, Teresa?" I asked.

"We should probably take them downstairs to my son's room and—" Before she could finish her sentence, Mark interrupted.

"Why don't you just take them to your boyfriend's house?" he yelled. She pretended not to hear him.

"Are you coming to the Halloween party at Danny's school Saturday?"

"Yes, I'm planning to."

"Are you going to wear a costume?"

"I hadn't planned on it. Do most parents?" Wearing

a Halloween costume as part of chaperoning Danny to his first school Halloween party was not on my list of priorities for the week.

"Lots of us do. I am going as a pirate wench," she said as she seductively strutted toward me.

"Being a pirate wench is the perfect costume for you," Mark shouted. "You won't have to dress up at all. You can just go as you are." They glared at each other.

A few weeks earlier I had attended Danny's school open house. Danny introduced me to Beth, his friend David's mom. He hasn't had David over to play yet and wanted to invite him. Beth and I discussed it and agreed she'd bring David over on Saturday. The next day she phoned.

"Hi Jake. This is Beth, David's mother. We met last night..."

"Hi, Beth. How are you?"

"Pretty good. Say, Jake, we have a problem with bringing David to play with Danny Saturday. Last night I forgot that David is sort of grounded so he can't go out this weekend. He knows about it and he understands," she sounded nervous.

"That's too bad," I replied. "Maybe we can do it the following weekend or another day after school. David seems like a great kid, and I know they've been trying to get together." There was a long pause.

"Jake, last night I went home and told my husband about you and Danny. This isn't personal, and I respect your honesty, but my husband isn't comfortable with our son coming to your home."

I have let Danny's friends' parents know I am gay. When I told Mark, he was a little taken aback but quickly suggested we go out drinking and perhaps I could help him pick up women. When I told another mom she laughed and said, "I already knew. This is a small community and word travels fast."

I live as an openly gay man. Several of Danny's friends, his teacher, his principal and all my friends know I am gay. If some parents have a problem with their child coming to our house, it's best that they find out from me—not through the small school rumor mill.

"I'm glad it isn't personal—" I started to say.

"It really isn't," she interrupted. "I respect you. I'm sure you're a great dad, but my husband isn't comfortable with David coming to your home. We are Christians, you know, and... I really do respect you—" her voice betrayed that this was not a comfortable call, "—and we'd be happy to have Danny come over here sometime if that's all right with you."

"Thanks. Maybe we can do that some day." We hung up. I felt angry, frustrated and rejected. I knew Danny would eventually face some of the same bigotry, prejudice and shame I've experienced, but I'd hoped it wouldn't happen so soon. *What if Danny doesn't want me to adopt him because I am gay? I don't want him to be teased for having a gay dad.* My head was spinning. I can't "hide" being gay. I tried that. It didn't work for many reasons including my need to strive to live with integrity and that being gay isn't shameful—it's just part of who I am.

Danny will always have a gay, recovering addict and Christian dad. Where we live he won't get teased for my love of Jesus. Most people are happy to learn that I don't use drugs and alcohol. But he will be taunted and teased because I'm gay. I haven't decided how to explain this to him. Sharing my opinion that some "Christians" are closed-minded, closeted bigots who don't understand the true message of Christ, or his example of unconditional love, probably isn't a good start. I want to teach Danny that this isn't his friend's fault. Many people are ignorant—if David's parents spent more time around gay people, they probably wouldn't be afraid of their son visiting our home.

When I began the adoption process, I expected to deal with Danny. I hadn't given much thought to interacting with his friends' parents or birth family. Danny's birthmother is gone. He hasn't seen her in many years, and he harbors resentment about her abandoning him and her other children. Danny's mother gave birth to at least seven kids, but there will never be a family photo of Danny and his sisters and brothers. They all have different fathers, except his older twin sisters, and their parents abandoned all of them. His visits with his birthfather were mostly limited to a prison visiting room. His closest emotional connections are to his maternal grandmother and his twin sisters.

Danny's 55-year-old maternal grandmother, Grandma Carol, is partly deaf, unable to work and lives in poverty. Her sole means of support is Social Security. About two years ago, his twin sisters, Ashley and Emily, left their foster home and moved in with their grandma's sister, Aunt Lisa.

Aunt Lisa was described by Danny's social worker as unpredictable and unreliable. For more than two years, Aunt Lisa regularly told Danny and his social worker that he could move in with her soon. When pressed by the state for a date she couldn't provide one. Immediately after Danny came to live with me, Aunt Lisa demanded a week-end visit with him. I objected and told his social worker it could be disruptive to our adoption and bonding process. The social worker agreed and the visit was denied.

In the meantime, Aunt Lisa told the state she was hiring an attorney to fight my effort to adopt Danny. I responded by proposing that all visits with Aunt Lisa and Grandma Carol be postponed until the adoption was finalized.

Last night I talked with Danny about his adoption. It felt important that he know that Aunt Lisa says she will take him now. I want to be Danny's dad, but I want him to live where he wants to be. If Danny chooses to live with his aunt, he gets to live with his twin sisters. That has been his dream since they were separated by foster care.

"Danny, I know this is really hard and you shouldn't have to think about this, but Aunt Lisa says she'll take you to live with her now."

"She's just lying," he interrupted. "She won't take me till I'm in seventh grade and easier to manage. That's what I heard her say..."

"I think she might really take you. I love you and I want to be your dad, but I am also your friend and I want to help you live in the best place for you. Do you remember when I said we both have to want to create a family together or I won't do it? It's time for you to think about what you really want. I'll love you either way, and I won't be mad at you."

"I don't want you to be my friend! I want you to be my dad. I need a dad!"

"I'd love to be your dad, but you need to make this decision yourself. You want to know a secret?" He nodded. "Who do you think is the expert on you? Who knows more about Danny than anybody?"

"You...?" he asked uncertainly. I shook my head. "My sisters?"

"Nope."

"My social worker?"

I laughed. "No, definitely not her."

"Who then?"

"You, Danny. You. Even though you're only ten years old, you are the expert on you. It's good to listen to other people's advice, but you have to learn to trust that somewhere inside, you know what's best for you. I don't mean that when you want to eat a quart of ice cream or five candy bars that's a good idea, but when it comes to the important things in life you have to learn to trust your own decisions. One way to do that is to pay attention to the still small voice of wisdom inside you that some people call God. Even though I will give you guidance, a good parent doesn't force their child to grow up the way they think they should be. A good parent teaches their son or daughter how to become who they really are."

"I don't know what you mean. How do I learn to be who I am?"

"It's hard to explain. Try imagining that all of us are born as a seed, and every seed creates a different plant or flower. Not all flowers look alike. Some flowers are red and smell wonderful and some are small and purple. I don't care what kind of seed you are, Danny. It doesn't matter to me. I just care that you grow up to be as beautiful as you can possibly be. The only advice I can give you is don't worry about my feelings. Don't worry about Aunt Lisa's feelings. Just choose to live wherever you believe is truly best for you."

"Well… I really want to live with my sisters," my heart sank but I kept my face calm, "but I have to do something good for me, Dad. I really need something to finally work out for me!" He started crying. "I want to stay here with you and Rusty!" he said between tears. "You're a loving dad, and you take good care of me. I have a nice home, and a good school with no gangs—and I don't want to change schools again—I want to be with you. I love you, Daddy. Please don't make me leave you and Rusty. I want to be home with you." His sobs grew louder as he hugged me. I patted his shoulder and caressed his neck as his tears moistened my cheek.

"Don't worry, Danny. If you want to stay with Rusty and me, I'll make sure you stay here."

"I don't want to tell Aunt Lisa—I don't want her mad at me." He looked panicked as he dried his tears.

"You don't have to, Danny. I'll tell her." I paid my attorney to attend Danny's next court hearing. I needn't have bothered. Aunt Lisa didn't mention the adoption, nor did she ask the judge to have Danny come live with her.

Chapter Sixteen

Sisters

Despite my misgivings about Grandma Carol and Aunt Lisa, state policy required (and I agreed), that Danny needed to have regular contact with his sisters. In Washington State, siblings separated in foster care are legally required to have visits at least twice monthly.[4] In July, I asked Louise to set up a visit for Danny and his sisters.

It took Louise three months to arrange it. In between, the children had no contact. At the last minute, Louise was unable to supervise the visit herself, so she arranged for a social worker who had never met any of the kids to fill in.

We agreed to meet at a diner near Seattle. I was nervous about meeting Danny's 15-year-old twin sisters, Ashley and Emily. Louise had insinuated to me that one of the girls was pregnant (as we spoke about his sisters, she said, "Danny's family is growing again, if you know what I mean") and I expected to meet sexually active, substance abusing, high school dropout teenagers.

When we walked in, both girls leaped up to hug Danny. It was as emotional as watching a family at the airport welcoming a veteran home. They all started crying. Danny's sisters adored him, and he basked in their hugs and affection. It was the happiest I had seen him—he almost glowed. After a few moments, Ashley turned to me and held out her hand.

"You must be Jake. I'm Ashley. Danny looks so good," her voice trembled. "Thank you for what you're doing for him. He's such a good kid and we love him so much— I can't thank you enough…" She choked up and simply smiled at me. I felt relief and gratitude flooding from her.

Her twin, Emily, rushed up and threw her arms around me. "Thank you for helping my baby brother," she said. I looked closely at both girls. Neither appeared pregnant. Both of them were nicely if inexpensively dressed, displayed impeccable manners and treated me like a well-loved uncle. I expected suspicion and resentment but experienced appreciation and love.

While Danny and his sisters played cards, I talked privately to the social worker. "Is one of the twins pregnant?" I asked.

She looked confused. I explained what Louise told me about the family growing and she replied, "Oh, Louise must have been referring to their birth mom. I heard she just had a baby boy born with Down syndrome who she abandoned at birth in a hospital in Texas."

I immediately liked both twins. As Danny shared his pictures of Rusty, his Alaska cruise, our trip to Disneyland and our home, they showed nothing but happiness for his good fortune. I had considered telling Danny not to bring his pictures, as I didn't want his sisters to feel jealous. He insisted they would want to see the photos, and he was right. There was no need to be concerned—both were guileless in their excitement for Danny's new life.

The two-hour visit passed quickly. We exchanged hugs and phone numbers, and then Danny and I drove home. On the ride back, Danny accidentally opened his camera, exposing the undeveloped film with the pictures he took of his sisters. He cried inconsolably. I knew his sadness wasn't just from losing the pictures—it was from the emotions of seeing and having to say good-bye to his sisters. I comforted him and assured him he would see them soon. A few hours later we arrived home.

"How do you feel about the visit, Danny?" I asked.

"Good. Sad."

"What do you mean?"

"It was good I finally got to see them, but I was really sad I had to say good-bye. Can they come up here and see me sometime, Dad? I want them to meet Rusty."

"Don't worry buddy. We'll see them again soon. You have really nice sisters," Danny beamed at me.

The next day I received a long email from Aunt Lisa. Instead of making unreasonable demands, she thanked me for my commitment to Danny. Though she expressed disappointment that Danny didn't get to live with her, she also wrote: *I have faith and believe that everything happens for a reason and feel much better knowing how much you've already done for Danny. Please know that I want more than anybody for Danny to be happy, feel wanted, loved and safe. He is very fortunate to have you and you've already done more for him than I could.*

Danny's social worker, Louise, convinced me Aunt Lisa was an unpredictable, unreliable influence on Danny. Yet the more I've worked with Louise, the less I trust her opinions and competence. The next day I discussed my confusion with my mother.

"It's weird, Mom. I started out thinking Aunt Lisa was a horrible person because of what Louise said, but now I am starting to question that. Those girls I met were great young women, and she can't be all that bad if she's raising them."

"There's another thing too, Jake," my mom replied. "She isn't that close a relative to those girls. She isn't their grandmother; she's their great-aunt. I'm sure she has some good qualities or she wouldn't have offered to raise them."

"Lisa wants us to come to her house for Thanksgiving. I think I'll go so Danny can have Thanksgiving dinner with his sisters."

"It works well for your father and me because we have

an opera in Canada on Thanksgiving night, and I was going to cancel it to have dinner with you and Danny. If you decide to go, we'll have our Thanksgiving dinner the next day."

As well as Danny is doing, I regularly see shadows of his past. He is frightened to be alone (he makes Rusty accompany him every time he goes upstairs), he sleeps with at least two lights on, most nights he asks to sleep in my bedroom, and he often cries when I leave him alone at night after reading to him. He hates any water splashing his face (he was tortured with hoses spraying his eyes and mouth when he was young), he is terrified that an intruder will "get him", he's extraordinarily easy to startle, he has no experience maintaining same-age friendships and is overly friendly with strangers. He often interrupts and tries to keep the attention and conversation focused on him. Every day Danny asks frequently if I love him.

Parenting is hard. It is forcing me to address behaviors and attitudes that I didn't know existed in me. It is humbling to realize how much I need to learn and grow to become a good father.

Chapter Seventeen

SLAP!

A few nights ago, I was at a charity auction. Seated at my table was Joann (the mother of one of Danny's classmates) and my neighbor Susan. Danny rides his bike up the half-mile gravel road to Susan's house to help feed and groom her horses.

"I think it's funny Danny is telling everyone he rode my horse to the mall," Susan laughed. "He has such a great imagination."

"What are you talking about, Susan?" I asked.

"Oh, Joann was just saying that Danny is telling the kids at school that he rode my horse to the mall."

"Has he ever even ridden your horse?"

"I've walked him around the pasture, but he hasn't ridden by himself." Susan noticed I seemed embarrassed. "Don't be upset. All kids lie, and it's kind of cute."

"It might be cute when he's ten, but it won't be cute when he's 15, and I'm still trying to help him learn how to make friends."

"Jake may have a point," Joann interrupted. "I overheard some of the kids say they're getting tired of all Danny's lies. I think he's funny," she said smiling at me, "but I don't think his lying is helping him any socially."

A few weeks ago, when my former partner Terry volunteered to take him roller-skating, Danny immediately fell and blamed the skates, insisting that the "wheels weren't tight enough." When Danny took the skates to get "adjusted," Terry overheard him ask the mechanic, "How do you roller-skate?"

My mom told Danny he needs to stop "stretching his blanket," a term she uses for exaggerating the truth. His stories include having a text-message exchange with Miley Cyrus about how lousy her music is, that he owns a 35-year-old parrot, that he attended second grade in Greece (or Holland after it featured prominently in his social studies report), how he beat up a professional wrestler, attended an Eminem concert, drove ATVs on logging roads, took a 28-foot boat out by himself on the Puget Sound, rode Susan's horse 11 miles to the mall and that Elvis Presley was his cousin.

The lies seem motivated by his insecurities. I remember feeling insecure when I was ten, believing I wasn't "good enough," and that if I knew a celebrity or had exotic experiences that other kids might like me. The irony is that if Danny didn't pretend to be someone he isn't, his natural kindness, compassion and enthusiasm would attract the friends he desires. Instead, his efforts backfire when he pretends to be someone he's not.

"Do you feel different from other kids, Danny?" I asked. I had just finished reading in bed to him.

"No…" he looked at me suspiciously. He knows I often talk to him seriously in his room at night.

"Really?" I asked skeptically. "You feel you're just like everyone else in your class?"

"Not everyone." I didn't say anything and kept staring at him. "FINE! I'm different, OK?" He glared at me.

"Do you think you aren't as good as other kids, Danny?"

"I'm not as good as the other kids, Dad," he whined. "I can't even do my math timings past four! I'm stupid—and other kids tease me because I don't know the rules at my school. How am I supposed to know the dumb rules when I didn't even go to this stupid school since first grade like all of them?" he hit his pillow. "I'm just a foster kid anyway," he looked away from me as he kept punching his pillow.

"Why do you think you're a foster kid?"

"Because I am." I didn't argue. After a few seconds he turned toward me, "Because I AM a foster kid!" he shouted.

"Hmmm. I thought you were being adopted and we were creating a family together. I'm not a foster parent, and this isn't a foster home, but I guess you can say you're a foster kid if you want—even though it's not true anymore."

"Well, I still can't do math…"

"But you're getting better at it, aren't you?"

"Yeah…"

"Danny, you're a great son. Lots of kids will do some things better than you, like math, and you'll do some things better than them, like building things. You've had a tough background. You're a new kid in school, you used to live in a foster home, and you had lots of bad things happen to you that aren't fair—"

"I know I have, and I don't want to talk about them," he interrupted.

Ignoring him I went on, "But that isn't your life now. You aren't a foster kid anymore; you have a tutor in math and you're getting better. What's more, you are a kind and loving boy and once people get to know you they'll want to be your friend.

"Not everybody," he protested.

"You're right, Dan, not everybody. You won't have everybody as your friend, none of us do, but you will have friends. Just be yourself—and don't tell the kids at school you rode Susan's horse to the mall."

"That was kind of funny," he smiled.

"It is kind of funny, but nobody believed you and it makes you look silly. How did you feel most of the time when you lived in foster care?"

"Sad, lonely and unloved."

"What do you think most kids in foster care need?"

"They need to be loved."

"How do you feel now that you aren't in foster care?"

"That I am in a good, loving family where someone

wants to take care of me and help me get a good education so I stay out of jail and have a good life."

"How does being loved make you feel?"

"It makes me really happy—it gives me my boost for the day."

"Is there anything I can do to make things better for you here?"

"No, Dad. Everything here is perfect. I love you," he hugged me tightly, kissed me and lay down on his pillow. As I left his room, I felt like his dad. Sometimes when I think about getting out of bed and beginning our daily routine, or leaving work early to pick Danny up from school, it feels as if he is an annoying visitor who has overstayed his welcome. But slowly, inexorably, I am starting to feel like his father.

The next morning Danny didn't wake up when I first called him. It took him almost 45 minutes to get out of bed and use the bathroom. His school starts at 9:25, and I can't drop him off before 9:10. We have to arrive within a 15-minute window before I can go to work. At 9, Danny was still upstairs wearing only his underwear, playing with Rusty and ignoring my deadline.

"Danny! Do you know what time it is?"

"Time to go?"

"Don't be a smart aleck! What have you been doing? You've had almost an hour to get ready, and you haven't even been downstairs to eat your breakfast!"

"I've been getting ready for school, Dad! Gosh! I don't

know what your problem is… I'm trying to hurry." I grabbed his arm and pulled him out of his bedroom and down the stairs. "Why are you hurting me?"

"I'm not hurting you. I'm taking you to school!"

"But I'm in my underwear!"

"So what. You can just go to school in your underwear today. Maybe next time that will help you think about how long you take to get ready!"

"Dad! I can't go to school in my underwear, everyone will laugh at me."

"You should have thought about that before you wasted all your time playing with Rusty," I kept pulling him toward the front door.

"Please, Dad! I'll hurry next time. I can get dressed quick! Please!" He looked panicked. Although I wasn't really going to take him to school in his underwear, I wanted to scare him.

"Come on. Hurry up. You need to put on your shoes."

"No! I'm not going!" He jerked his arm from me. "I FUCKING HATE YOU!"

CRACK! My hand slapped his cheek. By the time we both realized I hit him it was impossible to take it back.

"You hit me! You hit me! I can't believe I ever thought you loved me! You're just like all the rest of them!" Tears poured from Danny's eyes as he fled outside to hide in the woods. Rusty gave me a reproachful look as he followed Danny.

It was 9:15. I had an appointment at 10:00 and I didn't

know what to do. I called my attorney friend Franney, and she told me I needed to tell the social worker I hit Danny. I'd never hit a child in anger before. The feelings of guilt, confusion and shame were strong.

Danny came back in the house and quickly forgave me. There were no bruises, marks or welts on his face, and after the social worker asked a few questions she didn't seem overly concerned. But I was troubled. I thought I was a kind, loving, compassionate human being. How could I have slapped Danny?

When I spoke to a therapist friend about it, she said, "What I've seen in my practice is that kids who've experienced a lot of abuse often have what I think of as a psychic "kick me" sign on them. There is something about them that makes others want to hurt them. Now you're aware of it. Keep talking about it, and make sure when this comes up again—and it will—that you have a different strategy."

The more I thought about what happened, the more grateful I felt toward the adults who didn't hit me when I was a kid. I pushed many teachers, mentors, babysitters and relatives to their limits. Part of being a dad means learning not to hurt my child when I'm angry.

Chapter Eighteen

Medication

Being a parent is different than I expected. This shouldn't surprise me, as most significant life experiences don't reveal their complexity through imagination, but I thought I knew more about being a parent than I do. Being an uncle did not prepare me to be a father. Trying to subordinate my desires to meet the needs of my son can be hard.

Yesterday, Danny came to work with me because school was canceled due to snow. As we were leaving, my friend and co-worker, Chuck, said, "It's no wonder you're less patient with me since Danny moved in. You use up all your patience at home!" Chuck was right. Danny constantly barrages me with questions, commentaries, likes, dislikes and, "Hey, Dad, may I please have _____" (fill in the blank with "candy", "a snack", "a friend over", "a late bedtime", "video-game time" and so forth). The best thing is his behavior is becoming typical.

Thanksgiving with his Aunt Lisa and sisters went

well. The food wasn't my mom's or grandma's, everyone around the table but Danny was a stranger to me, the feeling that I was being evaluated by all the adults made me uncomfortable, but Danny was as happy as I've seen him.

Going to his Aunt Lisa's for Thanksgiving was my way of showing him and his sisters that I'm committed to their relationship. I intend to help them stay as close to each other as time and distance allow. The love they have for each other, and the maturity and encouragement shown us by his sisters made my decision easy.

I spent part of the day watching football. When Aunt Lisa started their tradition of singing karaoke Christmas carols together, I excused myself and went for an after-dinner walk. I could hear the sound of their amplified off-key caroling through the slightly cracked front window, and as endearing as it was for them, it simply affirmed that those voices and these people are not my family. I still enjoy Thanksgiving, but my grandma died in 1998, and it will never be the same holiday for me. Every Thanksgiving I remember my cousins, parents, siblings and grandparents and how it felt to be together with all of them at my grandma's house so many decades ago.

The Friday before Thanksgiving I went to Danny's parent-teacher conference. I asked my mom and dad to come. The previous week I finally received the results of Danny's testing and ADHD evaluation. His cognitive functions were all over the map. More and more it looked as if he has fetal alcohol spectrum disorder.

"Danny tries so hard," his teacher, Sarah, began. "I can see him struggling to work, but his attention drifts off quickly. Now that I have had him for a few months and he has settled down socially, I can see that his inability to focus is a significant disability for him. What do you think about trying medication again, Jake?" she asked.

I love Sarah. She is structured, experienced, compassionate and disciplined. She had a child with ADD, and she recognizes Danny's inability to focus as something he can't always control.

"I'm a little torn but I'm willing to try. I discussed this with Danny's psychiatrist, psychologist and therapist, and they suggest trying medication again now that he's living in a stable environment."

"I think it's a good idea to try it, Jake," the resource teacher interjected. "Every time I come in the classroom Danny's attention is somewhere other than where it's supposed to be. I know it's a hard decision, but you are truly trying to do what's best for him. No one here wants to medicate him just to make life easy for us." She turned toward my mother who was visibly uncomfortable, "What are you thinking?"

"It's just hard. I don't like medication, and I think far too often the schools encourage parents to overmedicate kids instead of trying to work with families to solve learning problems. I don't feel confident that this is the best thing for Danny," she said. My dad nodded in agreement.

"Everyone here agrees with you," the resource teacher continued. "But it's possible that this might be exactly what Danny needs so he can have the ability to focus—"

I looked toward both my parents. "Unless you strongly object, let's try it. We can give it a few weeks until Christmas break and then evaluate it. Danny's been on these drugs for years, but he's never had a permanent, loving home to go along with them. Because of Sarah's willingness to give feedback, I think it's worth a try."

My dad nodded in agreement. My mom didn't seem so sure. The next week I started giving Danny psychotropic medication again. A few days later his principal called, "Danny and another boy were working on a project, and Danny got frustrated and jabbed the other boy with a pencil."

"Did he poke him or stab him? Was there blood?"

"There were a few drops, but I wouldn't say he stabbed him. Danny seems sorry, and we have had problems with the other kid in the past. While I was clear with Danny this is serious, I don't think you need to be overly concerned."

When I picked him up after school, he could see I was angry. "What happened today, Danny?" He told me a convoluted story about needing a book for a social studies report and that the other kid shared the book with everyone but him. "So you basically stabbed another boy with a pencil because he wouldn't share a book?"

He shifted uncomfortably in his seat and softly answered, "Yes, Daddy." Danny whispers when he's ashamed.

"What was that, Danny? I couldn't hear you."

"Yes, I did…" he said a little louder.

"Is that appropriate behavior, Danny?"

"No…"

"I don't know what I am going to do for a punishment, but tonight after we get home from dinner at Grandma's, you're not allowed any TV or video games. I'll let you know what I'm going to do after I think about it."

"Are you still going to adopt me, Daddy?" I hadn't noticed Danny was trembling. He was afraid I would send him back to foster care. My heart hurt for him—no child should be afraid of losing his or her home for misbehaving in school.

"Of course I will, Danny," I assured him. "Getting in trouble in school has nothing to do with whether I am adopting you. Your behavior was inappropriate, but I love you and I don't expect you to be perfect. I know you're trying hard to change, and I appreciate it. I just feel disappointed that you stabbed that kid with a pencil."

"I'm sorry." Tears welled up and fell from his eyes. "I promise I won't do it again. You're the best daddy in the world, and I don't ever want to lose you."

That evening I sent a long email to his teacher, the resource teacher and the principal reminding them that

Danny was on psychotropic medication for the first time in three months and that a possible side affect is aggression.

Over the four-day Thanksgiving weekend, I took him off meds, made him spend a few hours in the yard raking leaves as a punishment, role-played how he could behave differently, and drilled four options into him to use when upset at school: walking away, signing out of class to go to the bathroom, asking his teacher for help, or going to the principal.

On Monday morning I gave Danny his medication again. At noon the principal called to inform me that Danny and three other kids had been sent to her office. A classmate had "accidentally" shoved Danny, and he retaliated by violently kicking the boy in front of the class.

I was furious when Danny came home, and I lost my temper. "I don't know what I am going to do," I yelled, "but if you're trying to put your adoption in jeopardy you're doing a damn good job of it!"

"Please, Dad! Please! I want to live here with you and Rusty—I love you, I'll be good!" As soon as I allowed my anger to bring up the adoption, I knew I had gone too far. I'm trying to bond with Danny and don't want to sabotage that because I'm angry.

"It's OK, Danny. I'm sorry. I shouldn't have said that. I'm going to adopt you. I'm just really upset by your behavior in school."

Two days later Danny put a sign on a kid that read "KICK ME," flipped off the entire class with his ring finger (not his middle finger), and argued with his teacher that he wasn't doing anything wrong. As a consequence, the school assigned Danny an in-school suspension. I decided to ground him to his bedroom for two days with no toys or electronics.

That night I opened his medication capsules and replaced the drugs inside with sugar. My research, my observation, and my intuition said the psychotropic medication Danny has been prescribed and forced to take since entering foster care is bad for him. When he came home from school I took him upstairs to his room.

"Come on, Danny, help me carry these toys out." When he moved in, I replaced his cardboard boxes and garbage bags with clear plastic totes for his toys. To help him resist the temptation of playing with his toys while grounded from them, I moved the totes to the hallway, leaving only two books, a pad and pencil in his room. He grabbed a tote and started bawling.

"Danny, it's just toys. You'll have them back in two days. You need some time to reflect on your behavior. Watching TV, building things in the garage and playing outside are privileges, and right now you haven't earned any privileges." He continued crying inconsolably. I usually encourage Danny to cry when he's sad, as I believe tears are a healthy way to express feelings, but this was too much. "Danny, quit crying. It isn't that big a deal."

"You're taking me back to foster care! I know you are! I HATE MY LIFE!" Suddenly I caught a glimpse of the scene through Danny's eyes. When he got in trouble in foster care, his foster parents packed his belongings in plastic garbage bags and cardboard boxes and sent him away. The first sign of moving was packing his clothes and toys. I realized he believed I was sending him away forever. I walked over to him, hugged him and stroked his hair.

"Danny, Danny," I murmured softly. "You aren't going anywhere. You made some poor choices, and now you have some uncomfortable consequences, but when you're in a real family you aren't sent away for getting in trouble— you're always a part of that family. I may not like your behavior, but I'll always love you."

"What if I burnt down the house or killed Rusty?"

"If you killed Rusty, I'd be very upset—"

"I would NEVER kill Rusty, Dad. I love him!" he interrupted.

"But, Danny, I know you aren't going to do those things. You're too kind, and even if you did something like that and went to jail, I'd still be your dad and I'd come visit you. I'd miss you very much, and I'd always love you. I'd probably even leave some money at the jail so you could eat some candy in your cell." He smiled.

"I love you, Dad. I'm really sorry about school." The weight of his arms pulled me toward him.

"I love you too. C'mon. We need to move your stuff out so you can start your punishment." That night I served him dinner in his room. I put ice cubes in his water and sprinkled a little Parmesan cheese on his pizza. He even got a small bowl of ice cream with a chocolate-chip cookie garnish for dessert.

The next day I received an unexpected phone call from the University of Washington fetal alcohol clinic coordinator. The UW is one the best resources in the world for diagnosis and treatment of fetal alcohol spectrum disorder (FASD). Unfortunately, they can only see a few kids each week. Demand is high and they are very selective. In September, I completed an initial application and a few weeks later learned that Danny was accepted for a full evaluation. The normal wait time is about a year. The reason the evaluation is so important is that the best practices for helping a child with FASD may be very different than those for a child with ADHD. Many FASD techniques involve learning coping skills, as those afflicted don't grow out of having FASD. The medication recommended can also be different. The psychotropic drugs Danny has been prescribed, while sometimes helpful for treating ADHD, may cause aggression in children with FASD.

The coordinator said that the UW was opening a satellite clinic in Everett and they had selected Danny to be one of the first two children to be evaluated there.

On Monday morning I was asked to come in for a meeting with Danny's teacher and principal. I asked his principal about her experience working at a school for behaviorally challenged kids.

"Do you think Danny would fit into a school like that?" I asked.

She paused to think about it. "I can see where some staff would recommend sending him there, but it would probably be the worst possible place for him. He'd likely absorb the behaviors of the other kids. Danny is in a perfect setting here. He has Sarah as a teacher—and that's gold—and we are going to continue doing everything we can to help him succeed. We have the rest of this year and next to really get him ready for middle school."

I shared with both of them about the fortunate timing of the UW evaluation, how the medication Danny has taken for years may cause aggression in children with FASD, and although I was concerned about his inability to focus, I was more concerned about his aggression when taking the medication.

"I think you should take him off the meds right away," Sarah suggested. "We tried it—it isn't working. Maybe we'll find something that can help him focus after the UW sees him, but what he's taking now definitely isn't helping him. Jake, I need to tell you he is very fortunate to have found you as a dad—there aren't many people like you around. I have great respect for you trying to help him, and I believe Danny is going to become a fine young man with your help."

"Thanks, Sarah. I feel the same way about you. Not to get too spiritual or anything, but I think all of us in his life are the exact people he needs right now. If I were paying $20,000 a year for private-school tuition, I couldn't be any happier with the school. He looks forward to coming here every day, and you seem to have the exact skills needed to help him. I don't believe any of this is a coincidence."

"I don't think it's a coincidence either," the principal offered. "Danny is where he needs to be, and we will find a way to help him. I am interested in the latest recommendations from the UW for working with FASD kids, so please share that with me after you've seen them and we'll do all we can here to support their recommendations."

I didn't tell them that Danny was already off medication and had been taking sugar placebos for the past five days.

Over the next week Danny grew calmer in class, started gaining his friends back and, although he continued to struggle with focusing he kept up with his classes and didn't assault anyone again. Last year he was permanently expelled from the regular school bus for choking and kicking a kindergartner and suspended for biting a kid in math, kicking a classmate in choir and punching a child in the lunchroom.

The reason Danny behaved violently in school wasn't a flaw in his character or development—it was a known side effect of the psychotropic drugs the state forced him to take since he entered foster care.

CHAPTER NINETEEN

NEGOTIATIONS

Earlier this week I had a tough day at work. One of my best customers went out of business, my company has been suffering from the poor U.S. economy, and our sales are down more than 50% for the year. Cutting costs and budgeting to stay profitable have been stressful.

The same day, I had a disappointing call from Margaret Swope, the state worker who negotiates adoption support. Danny's social worker had told me that he was entitled to receive money from the state to help with his special needs. Since I have to arrange for child care, tutoring, counseling and manage life as a single parent, I was looking forward to the financial assistance. Danny's previous foster parents received about $1,300 a month to take care of him.

"How much money do you think you need?" Margaret asked.

"I think we need the same amount as his last foster parents received, about $1,300 a month. I know the state spends a lot more than that on Danny now, but I believe you're limited to paying us no more than his last foster parents received. Danny has many issues, and within a month he is likely to have a diagnosis for fetal alcohol spectrum disorder from the University of Washington, so I believe the maximum is reasonable."

She was quiet a moment. "This program is for people who need it. I looked at your annual income; it's one of the highest I've seen. You don't need the money!"

"Whether I need the money isn't relevant. The money isn't for me. It's for Danny."

"But it's my job to use the money where it's needed most. I had a couple a few months ago where the wife earned no income and the husband earned less than $2,000 a year. This program made it possible for them to adopt—"

"If a couple earn only $2,000 a year, why are they adopting?" I interrupted. "What happens to that kid if you have to cut funding?"

She ignored me. "I have another couple with a child who needs extra money for feeding tubes…" she continued telling stories of people she believed needed the money more than we did.

"Look, I am not asking for food stamps. Obviously, I can support Danny with or without your help, but adoption support is supposed to encourage prospective parents by giving them resources when they adopt special-needs kids from foster care. When I adopt Danny, the state will save thousands of dollars a month. You probably spend three times more a month now than what I'm asking.

Washington State has an annual budget of over $500 million dollars to support around 10,000 foster children. Giving us $15,000 a year is a lot cheaper than what you're spending on Danny now. You'll save thousands of dollars every month till he turns 18."

"That's not how we look at it."

"I'm sure it isn't. Let me see if I have this right. If I take Danny as a foster child, the state will pay me $1,300 a month, pay for his clothes, medical insurance, all his other expenses, and I would have no responsibility for him—I can return him to the state if it doesn't work out. Is that right?

"Yes, that's correct."

"But if I adopt Danny and give him the permanent, loving home he needs, you want to give me nothing?"

"I didn't say 'nothing.' Based on your income, I couldn't offer you more than $250 dollars a month."

"So the state is offering me 80% less than what you'd give a foster parent to take care of Danny. Do I have that right?"

"The system isn't perfect," she protested. "The way you are describing it isn't the only way to look at it."

"I'm going to accept your offer. I love Danny, and I'm not going to postpone his adoption over $10,000 a year. I'll accept $250 a month—but this is wrong."

"The system isn't perfect," Margaret offered, sounding relieved to be done with me. "You can always renegotiate with us if your circumstances change. I'll have the papers drawn up before I leave for my vacation."

We made arrangements for me to sign and return the contract. I hung up the phone, still angry.

Bureaucracies may be a necessary evil, but when the state is willing to pay thousands of dollars a month to keep a child in foster care and little to nothing to encourage adoption of hard-to-place children in a permanent, loving home, the system is clearly broken.

When I got home I wanted to soak outside in the hot tub and enjoy the snow in the trees. But every time I use it, Danny tries to join me. He's afraid to be alone—he makes Rusty follow him everywhere—and even if Danny did his best to be calm in the hot tub, within minutes he would ask me where deer go to the bathroom, what time his bedtime will be when he turns 12, or how many pieces of candy he can buy with his allowance.

Since I needed some solitude, I told Danny I was taking a bath. I have a large whirlpool tub nestled in an alcove off the master bathroom. There is a broad tiled ledge with a small window looking out to the woods at one end and a smaller ledge with candles at the other. I drew a hot bath, turned out the lights, lit two candles, closed my eyes, breathed deeply, submerged into the hot water and tried to let go of my day.

The sound of the door latch creaking snapped me out of my solitude. Looking up, I saw Danny and Rusty standing in the bathroom.

"Hi, Dad," Danny said as he leaped up to the ledge at the end of the tub and sat cross-legged staring at me. "It sure is nice and quiet in here."

I sighed, "Yes, Danny, it is. What do you need? I am trying to take a bath…remember?"

"Oh, me and Rusty just wanted to check on you," he said giggling.

"Danny, I'm trying to relax. You don't need to be in here while I am in the bathtub. Please get out now!"

"OK, OK, I'm leaving, I'm leaving, but can I ask just one question? Please?"

"Do you promise you'll leave after that?"

"Yes, I will, Dad. Promise. Pinky swear." He lifted his crooked pinky toward me.

"Fine. What?"

"May I watch TV in your bedroom?"

"No! You should go downstairs. I'm still trying to take a bath."

"But I'm scared, Dad. It's dark and cold…" he whined.

"Fine, just shut my door and you can wait on my bed. No TV though!" I tried to relax, but the water was cooler now and serenity eluded me.

Less than a minute later he called out, "Are you almost done, Dad? I'm bored…"

I knew I could either be angry or amused. I laughed. "Yes, Danny, I'm almost done."

The next day when I told my sister about it, she said, "Oh, you messed up. You have to lock the door and tell him if he isn't bleeding he can't interrupt you." If I didn't have the support of my friends and family, I couldn't do this. Thankfully, the resources I've needed to adopt Danny have appeared when I needed them.

I've read thousands of pages of case notes, medical records, legal records and mental health records, and perhaps the most important thing I've learned from them is that Danny needed me the day I appeared. Even a month later might have been too late.

CHAPTER TWENTY

FIRST CHRISTMAS

Despite bad past experiences, Danny is optimistic about our first Christmas together. At his grandma's house, Danny had learned to cloak a towel around his presents under the tree, in order to capture the silverfish, earwigs and cockroaches that hid in the dark paper crevices of the wrapped gifts.

At the "short-term" foster home Danny lived in for two years, he wasn't allowed out of his room on Christmas Day. "No one wants your sorry ass messing up Christmas!" his foster mom, Ms. Benedict, told him. Danny was served cold leftovers in his bedroom with the door shut. A camera in the hall and an alarm on his door alerted her if he left his room.

As memories of his past holiday experiences trickled out, I wondered if Danny was exaggerating, but it soon became obvious that Danny wasn't abused and neglected just by his birth family; his foster mother and the state betrayed him too. I asked one of his social workers a few questions about Ms. Benedict.

"Why was Danny stuck in a short-term foster home for almost two years? Wasn't he supposed to be there just a few weeks?"

She sighed, "It was a bad situation. The placement people claimed they had nowhere else to put him. He was diagnosed as an extremely troubled eight-year-old, and over time it looked as if he had bonded with her and she asked to keep him."

"Danny said that she locked him in his room and gave him a bucket to pee in. That couldn't be true, could it?"

"I don't know about the bucket, but it's true she locked him in his room. She was told it was against department policy and unsafe to lock children in their bedrooms, and she agreed to stop."

"Danny said that after she took the permanent lock off his door she used a removable lock to keep him in his room like a cell."

"He never said that to us, but I'll admit I never liked that woman. She gave me the creeps. I thought she was a terrible fit for Danny, but we were told there was no-where else to put him and we kept working with his aunt to move him in with her and his sisters. You know how well that worked out!"

"Did he improve at all in Ms. Benedict's care?"

"No, there wasn't any consistent improvement."

"What really bothers me is that if Danny had

significantly improved, the state would have reclassified him from a level-four to a level-three foster child, right?"

"Yes, that's true. If his behavior significantly improved, his classification would have changed."

"So instead of getting $1,300 a month for Danny, Ms. Benedict would have received $300 a month less if Danny improved to a level three, and $600 a month less if he improved to a level two.[5] The more Danny's behavior improved, the less money Ms. Benedict would receive for taking care of him. Her financial incentive was to make sure Danny never got better!"

"I haven't heard it described that way before, but you're right. It doesn't make sense."

Ms. Benedict was so obese that good hygiene eluded her. Danny didn't like being near her because she stank. She forced him to wear diapers every night, never went to his school or sports activities and "attended" his school conferences by telephone. She was able to competently cash her $1,300 a month check for being his foster mother.

Through the holiday season, Danny and I joked about having a "Benedict Christmas." A Benedict Christmas meant no gifts, no one who loves you, no candy and no Christmas dinner. As the chocolates in Danny's advent calendar slowly disappeared, I decided it was time to quit singing about the Benedict Christmas.

"Why don't we start singing about a white Christmas, Danny?" I asked. "I'm getting tired of the Benedict Christmas."

"We could sing about a Danny Christmas," he suggested.

I was intrigued. "What's a Danny Christmas?"

"I don't know..." he looked thoughtful.

"You brought it up... I'm curious. Tell me what it looks like. Just imagine it in your head, look around, see who's there and describe it to me..."

"OK. Well, I see you and Rusty, my sisters, Grandma and Grandpa, and a big ham, lots of cheese, tomatoes, olives, and candy."

"Are there any gifts?"

Danny grinned, "Yes, Daddy, there are!" He started jumping up and down. "There are lots of gifts for ME!"

"Are there any gifts for anyone else?"

His jumping slowed a little, "Yes, Daddy, there are some for YOU!" he shouted as he leaped and hugged my neck. Now that he weighs 90 pounds, landing on me hurts more. "There are lots for you from me. I love you, Daddy!"

"Anything else? How does it look outside?"

"There's snow. Lots of snow. I've never had snow at Christmas, Dad."

Danny got his wish. Two weeks before Christmas it started to snow. Within days our yard had two feet of snow. Three weeks later it finally began to melt.

There was so much snow on the ground that the state patrol and county sheriff had asked everyone to stay home, as most roads weren't plowed or safe. At 5 a.m. the Monday before Christmas, the phone rang. The novelty of the phone ringing so early jolted me awake.

"Hello?" My voice was cracked and groggy.

"Jake… Jake, it's your friend Patricia. I hope I didn't call too early… we have to be at the airport at 6:30 a.m. Can you still give us a ride?"

The memory of strolling on a balmy Halloween night trick-or-treating with our kids six weeks ago, and casually agreeing to drive Patricia, the mother of one of Danny's friends, to the airport for Christmas slowly seeped into my brain.

"Gosh, Patricia, I forgot all about that. I don't know… the roads are pretty bad… do you think we can make it there? I don't even know if any planes are flying."

"I think so. I'm sorry I didn't call you last night to remind you… It was pretty late and I didn't want to wake you." Despite wanting to say there was no way I was getting out of bed on a 20-degree morning and driving through 15 miles of snow to take her to the airport, she had watched Danny the past Thursday and Friday when school was canceled. We both knew I owed her.

"I'll be there as soon as I can. I'll call you if I can't get out of the driveway." It took ten minutes to drive two miles to her house. When I arrived she was struggling to get her kids out of the door with their luggage and gifts.

As she got in my car, she pointed to my tires. "Are those snow tires?"

"No, they're just all-weather. Fortunately I bought new ones last week, so at least they have good tread."

"Oh, I just got new snow tires for my car and they're

good! I can cross all the mountain passes—I just love them. You might want some for your car," she suggested.

Her car was sitting next to my truck under eight inches of snow. She called me for a ride so she could avoid paying to park at the airport! It was a bad way to start my week.

I spent much of the rest of the week driving through snow. On Christmas Eve, Danny and I went to my mom's house for dinner, and we followed that with my family's tradition of Dad reading the Christmas story from Luke before opening some presents. It was the last Christmas for my parents in their house (they had bought a condominium in an over-55 community), so it was especially nostalgic for me to enjoy my mother's meal and to listen to my dad reading the Bible on Christmas Eve.

Terry had intended to go to eastern Washington to be with his dad but decided to stay in town because of the snow. After we left my parents, he came home with Danny and me to spend Christmas morning with us. When Danny went to bed, Terry helped me be Santa Claus. It felt strange to be the person creating a child's Christmas experience.

Christmas morning Danny awoke to a tree full of gifts and a toy train from Santa. Opening presents took a long time. Danny had about 15 packages under the tree. He didn't expect many gifts and is pleased by a toy from a fast-food restaurant or a new pair of socks. When he unwrapped a package containing a Slinky, he stopped, took out the Slinky, carried it to the top of the staircase, watched it walk down and kept encouraging Terry and me to enjoy it with him. When he opened a tool belt and tools, he spent five minutes putting on the belt, adjusting it, fitting on his safety goggles and examining each tool.

Terry and I kept giving each other questioning looks. Both of us were used to opening a gift, giving it a cursory inspection and moving on to the next one. Danny savored each package. It took more than two hours to open his presents, and each one was a new delight. A little before noon my friend Leslie arrived. We had made plans to have Christmas dinner with my parents, her son Nolan and his girlfriend.

Shortly before dinner, Nolan's girlfriend came bursting into the house. "Hurry, hurry! There's been an accident!" She was really upset, and I ran out the door. Nolan and Danny were lying on the ground in the snow. Nolan's all-terrain vehicle was next to them. Danny was loudly moaning.

"What happened?" I shouted.

"They were riding the ATV on the driveway and Danny was sitting in front of Nolan. They tried to stop but they smashed into the back of my truck! Are they all right?" I noticed a giant dent in her tailgate. The taillight was smashed, and shards of red plastic were scattered like broken Christmas ornaments across the white snow.

"I don't know. Are you OK, Nolan?"

"I think so," he answered. "How's Danny?"

"Help me, Dad. I'm really hurt. OH!" Tears were

streaming down his face, and he looked scared. We got him in the house and pulled off his pants. A purplish bruise extended from his upper thigh to mid ankle. My mom and Leslie put ice on him, and I checked his pupils for any sign of a concussion. After 15 minutes, it appeared he didn't need to go to the emergency room.

Nolan had offered to let Danny drive the ATV in the driveway. Somehow Danny's glove got stuck in the accelerator. He couldn't stop and ran into the back of the parked truck. Danny lost his index fingernail and had an extraordinary bruise for weeks.

Our first Christmas together wasn't as festive or calm as I would have liked. The snow was more of an inconvenience than a blessing (though it was beautiful and Danny did enjoy a white Christmas), but I got to share it with people I love. And somehow, by the end of the day, it felt like my first Christmas as a real dad.

CHAPTER TWENTY-ONE

ADOPTION SUPPORT

A few days after Christmas, Danny's sisters Ashley and Emily came for a two-night visit. A little after midnight on their first overnight, Danny came running into my room.

"Dad, Dad! The spektip system quit working! Hurry!"

"Do you mean the septic system? What are you talking about?"

"HURRY, DAD! HURRY!" He tugged my hand toward the bathroom door. Water was pouring from the overflowing toilet bowl and flooding the floor. I immediately turned the water off.

"See, Dad? The drain is full!"

"Actually, Danny, the toilet is clogged. I think the septic system is fine. Did you put anything in it?"

"Nope, just poop and toilet paper."

"If this ever happens again, Danny, please don't keep flushing the toilet. Just flush it once and if it doesn't drain, don't try flushing it again. Turn the valve off like I did, and come get me."

"I'm sorry," he looked crestfallen. "I thought if I kept flushing it, it might work."

"It's all right, you didn't know. Just don't do it again." There were gallons of water on the tile floor. I cleaned up the mess and discovered I don't own a plunger. In the four years I have lived here, I hadn't needed a plunger before. I put a "DO NOT USE" sign on the bathroom door and went back to bed. The next morning I got a plunger and cleared the clog.

A few weeks later it happened again.

"Dad! Dad! The toilet stopped again. I only flushed it once though!"

"Good job, Danny. Let me see." I went to the bathroom and saw almost half a roll of toilet paper in the toilet bowl. "Danny, why is there so much toilet paper in here?"

He shrugged. "I don't know."

"Well, who does know? Didn't you put it there?" He nodded. "Do you usually use this much?" He nodded yes again as his eyes averted from the toilet bowl. "Danny, I am really glad you're using toilet paper, but you need to use about four or five squares at a time and fold it like this," I said, demonstrating.

"OK," he meekly replied. I scooped the soggy toilet paper out of the basin and cleared the clog.

After the snow melted, Danny's school was closed

several days because of roads flooding. He hadn't attended three consecutive days of class in more than a month. It was hard to plan to go to work not knowing if he would go to school.

Danny's adoption was supposed to be completed on January 19th. I had done everything I could to adopt him as quickly as the law allows. All the requirements and paperwork were complete except my contract with the state for adoption support. While a support agreement isn't required to complete an adoption in Washington, it had to be agreed upon prior to the adoption or Danny would lose the opportunity to receive adoption support forever.

I initially had agreed to accept the $250 a month the state offered, but the other adoptive parents I spoke to all received more. Although the state is experiencing severe budget pressures, their financial trouble shouldn't be Danny's problem. He deserves to receive as much assistance as other children.

Our adoption support representative, Margaret, said that if I didn't return my signed contract to her before Christmas, I couldn't complete Danny's adoption in January. On Christmas Eve, I went to my office to mail it. I wanted the child-welfare system out of our lives as soon as possible. I had spent $95 on a used book about adoption support,[6] but delivery was delayed because of the snow. It arrived Christmas Eve.

I already felt Margaret was manipulating me, and my gut told me that signing the contract was unwise. I decided to delay returning the adoption support agreement until I read the book. I quickly learned the state misled me. Adoption support is partially federally funded, and federal law prohibits the state from using my income, or an "economic means test" to determine the amount of Danny's monthly payment. Danny's needs, not my financial resources, are supposed to be the main factor for determining how much he receives.

A good child advocate stands firm on the need for adoption support, as the money is for the child's benefit. I wrote Margaret an email explaining that I changed my mind, $250 a month was unacceptable, and I had to postpone Danny's adoption until we came to an agreement. She responded by scheduling a meeting with her and her supervisor.

A week later, I drove 60 miles to meet them at the regional office. I walked in with a large file box of indexed notes and three-ring binders containing over 2,000 pages.

"What's all that?" Margaret asked. She looked at me as if I had brought a dog to a cat party.

"Some of my files on Danny. I didn't know what I'd need today and was hoping we'd get some resolution."

"You certainly won't need all that," she huffed. She only had two inches of files on the conference table and seemed to suffer from file envy.

Throughout the negotiation, Margaret glared at me with her arms crossed. As we talked, she or her supervisor constantly reminded me that not everyone chooses to receive adoption support and that someone with my financial resources, in their opinion, shouldn't ask for it. They subtly implied adoption support is a welfare program like food stamps or free school lunch instead of an entitlement program like Social Security.

After half an hour, the supervisor asked, "Why are you asking for adoption support when you indicated in your home study you can meet all of Danny's needs?"

"I can meet all of Danny's needs."

"Then why are you asking the state for the maximum adoption support payment when your home study admitted you can meet all of Danny's needs yourself?" She and Margaret exchanged a triumphant look.

"As you know, Danny has a long list of special needs, and the state has classified him as a level-four foster child. I do have the financial ability to meet Danny's needs, but that has nothing to do with his right to receive adoption support. As you should know, adoption support is not a welfare program. It's a state and federal incentive to encourage adoption of special-needs kids. It's more like receiving Social Security than applying for food stamps. I'm requesting it because Danny is entitled to it." Margaret glared at me.

"But we see financial resources like yours in fewer than

1% of our adoptions. Do you really, truly, believe someone with your resources should be considered for the same amount of support as a family earning $20,000 a year?" the supervisor asked.

"No, I don't. Actually, I think I should receive more—that would be fair."

She looked shocked, "More! Why should you get more?"

"It'll cost me more to integrate Danny into my life. I'll take him skiing with me, buy him a mountain bike, go horseback riding, visit my family in California, take him to Disneyland, buy him braces and lots of other things I couldn't afford if I earned $20,000 a year. He'll want an iPod like his friends, name-brand tennis shoes and all sorts of other things I would never consider if we were struggling financially. Since I'm fortunate enough to have a good income, I'll spend much more on Danny than if I earned less. Therefore, I should receive more." Margaret looked at me as if I were a devil.

"That's not the standard we use to determine adoption support payments," Margaret said coolly.

"Well, you should. You're supposed to consider how adoption support and my resources combine to meet Danny's ordinary and special needs. That's exactly what the law says. The state did a horrible job of finding foster homes for Danny, and I'm not doing my job if he doesn't get all the resources available to help him now."

After an hour of going back and forth, it was obvious

we weren't going to reach a compromise. "I suppose you know that if we can't reach an agreement, I have a right to a fair hearing," I said.

"He does?" Margaret blurted out in surprise.

"Actually, yes, I do," I replied, as I pulled out a packet of information about fair hearings.[7] Margaret looked stunned. "I hoped we wouldn't get to this point, but I think any more discussion is pointless and I'd prefer that a judge review the facts and determine who's right. You claim Danny isn't entitled to a larger adoption support payment than $250 a month because I have too many financial resources. I believe that's an illegal means test."

"No, your salary isn't being considered, only your other financial resources," the supervisor objected.

"That's still an economic means test."

"That's your opinion."

"Yes, it is, and since we can't agree, let's have a judge decide. If I'm mistaken, I'm sorry. But I don't think I am or I wouldn't pursue this. In the meantime, I won't adopt Danny until this is resolved. I'm sorry his adoption is delayed because child-welfare services can't follow federal guidelines for adoption support."

Fighting bureaucracy is draining. I'm trying to adopt a special-needs child, but negotiating with the adoption support representatives felt like a hostile interrogation from suspicious police detectives. Their attempts to use guilt, false facts and aggressive negotiation tactics don't sit well with me.

It takes time, money, persistence, patience and, for me, a desire to make the path easier for the next person who comes along. If it were just for me, it wouldn't be worth all the effort. It would be easier to accept the lower payment and not spend so much energy fighting the state.

It's discouraging that the agency that should be encouraging Danny's adoption, the Washington State Department of Social and Health Services, is delaying his adoption through their own bureaucratic incompetence. Sadly, it isn't surprising. Much of what I've seen in the child-welfare system is not in the best interests of the children—it's about social workers and supervisors not taking chances, protecting their salaries and trying not to get sued. Bureaucrats rarely get in trouble for saying "no," but saying "yes," even when it is in the best interests of a child, can carry unknown risks.

I expect to win this fight, but adopting Danny will take more time. The law requires the hearing process to move quickly, but even though government agencies use laws and policy to force citizens to meet deadlines, state workers don't always observe the same standards themselves.

Chapter Twenty-Two

Good News

Living in the 21st century, surrounded by cell phones, fuel-efficient cars, Internet shopping and too many television channels, it is easy to overlook the dragons that need slaying and to believe that David and Goliath are a myth.

The dragons today may not be covered in rugged green scales, but they still breathe fire and can kill you. Every culture and every government silently witness David and Goliath fighting daily. Too often David loses, limping away with a sore arm, disillusioned soul and an empty wallet.

Today David won.

This afternoon, a week after my meeting with Margaret and her supervisor, I received an email that the state will pay a little over $1,000 a month in adoption support for Danny until he turns 18. When I read the email over again and realized what it meant for us, a lump grew in my throat. Three things occurred to me simultaneously: I knew my uncertain decision to fight the state was the best thing for Danny (his adoption was delayed six weeks, but he is being compensated with an additional $66,000 in tax-free adoption support), I knew Danny would legally be my son within a few weeks, and I grieved for the other adoptive parents, who need adoption support resources for their own special-needs children but aren't able to stand up to the child-welfare system.

Two months ago I knew nothing about the adoption support program. I got advice from my dad, a few friends and my brother. I hoped that my decision to fight the state was the best thing for Danny, but I still had doubts. Today's victory gives me hope that an inexperienced citizen armed with knowledge, conviction, willingness to fight and good motives can still slay a dragon.

Though I am glad for Danny, my heart aches for the other kids who don't get what they need because they have no one to fight for them.

Our adoption journey is coming to an end. A few days ago, we were looking at photos from last summer.

"Who's that, Danny?" I teased as I pointed to a picture taken the first day I picked him up at his foster home. We both stared at a smiling, overweight, middle-aged man standing next to a small, anxious, thin boy. Danny's arms were cocked at his waist in a vain attempt to look older. He wore an ill-fitting gray shirt, shoes too small, pants too large and a military-style crew cut.

"I don't know," he smiled. "I don't even know who that is—"

"It's us! That seems like a long time ago, doesn't it, Danny?"

"I don't want to remember that anymore, Dad." He looked sad.

"Yeah, I know. There are things I don't like to remember either, but even in the bad times I've found stuff that helps me. Remember how I told you I lived in a group home when I was 16?"

"Yeah…"

"The group home sucked. I hated living there. But because I lived there when I was a kid, it helps me understand what it might have been like for you to live in foster care. What I am trying to say is that I've learned a lot from the times that were hard for me. I think if I didn't remember my own hard times I might not have adopted you."

"Really, Dad?"

"Yep. Remember how everyone used to get mad at you for stealing food in foster care?"

"Yeah…"

"I didn't really worry about that because I used to steal food too. When I was young, I really liked sugar—"

"You still do!" he interrupted.

"And I know what it's like to live somewhere and not get food when you're hungry. It was like that for me in jail and sometimes in the Army. That's why when you came to live with me I let you keep goldfish crackers in your nightstand."

"But, Dad, I don't even need them anymore!"

"I know, Danny—that's the point. You don't need them anymore."

The progress Danny has made can't be attributed to any one person. From the beginning, unseen forces have guided and cleared our path. Every time I wanted to quit and abandon him, I was inspired to keep going. The evidence of providence abounds. I see it in his teachers, in how he relates to others and mostly in how he has changed. Danny isn't the same kid—he looks different, he sounds different, but most of all he feels different.

The obstacles from the state continue. Yesterday his local social worker called to schedule a monthly health and safety visit.

"How would Thursday be after school?" she asked.

"Not very good. Danny's adoption is in Tacoma the next day and we have to drive down the night before. Can't his regular social worker see him before court and have that be the monthly visit?"

"No, I need to see him up here. Sometimes our rules don't make a lot of sense," she sympathized.

"But he's being adopted the next day! We both know it's a waste of time to schedule a routine safety visit the day before his adoption."

"I know. I'm really sorry. But our policy is we have to see each kid monthly, and we're under strict orders from the bigwigs to improve our statistics. I have to see Danny tomorrow before you go."

"Fine," I said, resigned. "I'll bring him to your office after school on the way to Tacoma."

The foster-care bureaucracy moves along like a blind elephant, spending too many resources where they aren't needed and too little where they are.

A few weeks ago, Danny was evaluated at the University of Washington for fetal alcohol spectrum disorder (FASD). A team of psychiatrists, physicians, social workers and psychologists poured over hundreds of pages of records. They tested Danny, and they interviewed me. The UW makes an FASD evaluation using four primary criteria: birth size, physical characteristics, central nervous system damage and the birthmother's drinking history. Each area is ranked from one to four. The lower the number, the less likelihood of having FASD. Danny's mother's drinking history was assigned a four; there is ample evidence she drank in her pregnancy. His birth size was a one; he was an average-size child. His physical anomalies were a three; meaning there are enough characteristics of FASD that it is significant.

The diagnosis of FASD hinged on the extent of damage to his central nervous system. This is often the hardest area to evaluate. Danny was diagnosed with ADHD and was extensively tested in second, fourth and fifth grades. The psychologist at the UW also performed additional tests during the evaluation. Based on the testing and his ADHD diagnosis, I suspected Danny would be rated a three, which combined with his mother's drinking history and physical characteristics means he has FASD.

After the tests and interviews, Danny and I waited in the lobby for an hour as the team discussed his case. The clinic's social worker finally came to get us. "Jake, can you and Danny please come back with us now?" I felt anxious as she directed Danny to a supervised play area, and I followed her to a conference room where the staff was seated around a large table. "Have a seat," she said indicating the head of the table.

"Danny is a delightful young man. You have done a remarkable job with him. The good news is that Danny does not have FASD. He does have physical characteristics and central nervous system damage consistent with fetal alcohol exposure—but we are very optimistic about his ability to overcome his challenges."

For an instant, I was disappointed he didn't have FASD. I was sure he had it, but I immediately recognized that my feeling was as foolish as being disappointed by a doctor confirming a benign tumor.

"You're sure he doesn't have FASD…?"

"Yes, we're sure." A wave of relief washed over me. "We will give you a full report with all our findings. He does have some significant problems, and he was definitely fetal alcohol exposed, but we believe the resources you and his school are providing will be able to meet most of his needs."

He doesn't have FASD. He doesn't have FASD. HE DOESN'T HAVE FASD! I started to feel chills of joy run down my spine. I had worried that as his peers grew up Danny might remain an immature ten-year-old. I was afraid he might need assisted living, that he might never leave home, be able to make good decisions or learn to manage his impulsivity.

"What about his ADHD and emotional problems?" I asked.

"Danny definitely has some problems, but he also has great strengths. One thing we noticed in our testing is that when he couldn't solve a spatial reasoning problem he developed alternative strategies on his own to reach a solution. He's very creative. Another thing all of us observed is how well he is doing with you. Every report we received from his therapists, social workers and school comment on how well he is doing in your care. Wasn't he suspended five times last year from school?"

"It was actually nine."

"And this year he hasn't been suspended at all. We noted that you took him off medication, and he seems to be doing better. For a child with FASD, a change in environment wouldn't result in such a dramatic improvement in behavior. We expect to see similar problems no matter what environment he lived in. With Danny, it is clear that when you gave him a loving home and he bonded with you as his parent, many of his problems went away. You should feel good about the difference you've made in his life."

"I've done what I can. But he has the best teacher in the world, and my friends have been wonderful—some of them have practically adopted him themselves. But mostly, the credit has to go to Danny—the way I see it, God gave Danny a lifeboat and he has chosen to jump into it—I'm so proud of him…" I choked up and couldn't say any more.

The clinic director hadn't spoken yet. She looked at me kindly and said, "Jake, I see how much you love him. I want to share something with you. I've been doing this for many years and I've seen hundreds of children, many of them foster children like Danny, who have experienced horrible trauma and abuse, first in the womb, and then after they're born. FASD is rarely an isolated disease. It comes in conjunction with all sorts of environmental and behavioral concerns. In all the years I've done this, I've rarely, if ever, seen anyone come to us as prepared as you were—all your files were thorough and complete—and who is such an advocate for a foster child."

"I want to do what I can for him because I'm trying to behave like a good dad—" I interrupted.

"The reason all of us believe Danny is going to be all right is not just because of his many strengths," she continued. "That's only a part of it. The bigger piece is you. Your influence in Danny's life is what makes the difference. Some day things may become much harder than they are now. Danny will grow up and become a teenager. He is likely to rebel at times, and he's at risk for substance abuse and juvenile delinquency. He could have a hard time dealing with everything he has suffered. But you'll be there. Supporting him, taking care of him and always loving him. I want you to know how much I admire the effort you are making for this young man. Always remember that you're doing a remarkable job. He is a very lucky young man to have found you."

As the heads around the table nodded in agreement, I let the gratitude in the room flow through me. Soon I'll legally be Danny's father, but today I know I already am.

Chapter Twenty-Three

Adoption Eve

On the surface, the week preceding the adoption appeared typical. There was choir practice on Wednesday, breakfast every morning at eight, frequent requests for candy, bedtime stories, well-rehearsed stalling techniques at bedtime, hugs and school. Despite the superficial veneer of ordinariness, both Danny and I grew edgy as adoption day approached.

I felt distracted at work and procrastinated performing mundane accounting tasks and returning phone calls. Danny was tense, and his behavior wavered between hyper and infantile. He whined in the morning about the cereal I gave him. If I gave him milk, he wanted juice. If I gave him juice, he wanted milk. On Wednesday after school, he ran around the house, leaped over the back of the couch, landed on his head and started crying. I knew it was time to talk.

"Danny?"

"What!" He knew he had done something wrong.

"Why are you doing somersaults over the couch? They aren't toys. They're furniture, and I don't want you ruining them."

"I'm NOT doing somersaults, Dad. I am DIVING over them and trying not to touch them. See?" He started to leap over the couch again.

"Danny! Stop it. Do NOT jump on the furniture. Don't even touch it!"

"But, Dad, then I can't even sit down! That's not even fair!" Tears fell and he looked helpless.

"That's not what I meant. You can sit on the couch, but you can't play on it."

"But you said I couldn't touch it… and if I sit on it I AM touching it."

"You know what I meant. It came out wrong. I meant don't play on the furniture. Come sit down so we can talk." He looked at me suspiciously and sat just beyond arm's reach at the far end of the couch. "You can come closer…" He scooted a few inches toward me and then looked away. "Eye contact, please…"

"Fine," Danny glared at me as if I were a drill sergeant disciplining him with push-ups.

"What's going on, buddy?"

"Nuthin'…"

"I have something going on. I'm nervous about the adoption. It's only two days away."

Children in foster care are victims of neglect,

abandonment, abuse or all three. Over time they develop a finely honed sense of when their home, school or environment are shifting. The average foster child has had at least three different homes[8] while in foster care and usually numerous respite (weekend or weeklong temporary homes) stays. Every time they move, they need to adjust to a new bed, new rules, new meals, new authority figures, and to try to make friends all at once.

"Why? What's wrong, Dad?" Fear exuded from him. He sensed his world shifting again and was afraid I might not adopt him. Instead of expressing his fears, Danny was hiding them. He didn't want to appear vulnerable—he wanted me to like him—so he was repressing his feelings and trying to please me.

"Danny, what's wrong?" He looked shocked and didn't reply. "C'mon Dan... what's wrong? Are you afraid I won't adopt you?" He didn't answer. Tears began falling down his cheeks as he nodded yes. I reached out and held him. "Danny, Danny," I murmured. "It's OK. I'm not going anywhere. Nothing is going to stop me from adopting you, and we're going to have a real family."

"I don't want to go back to foster care," he blurted between tears. "I just want to be 'dopted and have a loving family." I gently pushed him back.

"Look into my eyes, Danny. What are the eyes?"

"The windows to the soul," he sniffled. I have worked with him for months at reading people by looking in their face and eyes. To practice, I lie to him obviously and let my eyes reveal I'm not being truthful. Danny has become good at reading me. Now when he wants to know if I am telling the truth, he orders me to look in his eyes.

"That's right. What do you see when I tell you I love you and I'm going to adopt you?" I looked in his eyes with all the love I could muster.

"The truth. That you want to adopt me."

"You're right, Danny. I'm just nervous because I haven't been a dad before. There's only one way I'm not adopting you Friday."

"What's that?" he interrupted, looking scared.

"If you don't want to. The only reason I won't adopt you is if you don't want to."

"But I want you to adopt me!" he said, relieved.

"Then you'll be adopted," I smiled at him, and he hugged me. "Now go finish your homework, and then we can play a video game."

"I love you, Daddy." He smiled at me as he went to the kitchen table to work on his math.

Our adoption in Tacoma was scheduled for Friday morning at nine. Rather than risk being late, I booked a hotel room for the night before. When I asked Danny whom he wanted at his adoption, he listed many family and friends. I explained most of them would have a hard time missing work or school, but we could have a celebration dinner with them in Anacortes. He narrowed down his list to his sisters and a few close friends. Though

I would have liked my parents (who were in Utah) or
siblings (who live everywhere but Washington State) to
be there, I was comfortable not pressuring any of them
to come. All my friends and family have ended up being
incredibly supportive, and the time we will spend together
in the future is more important than an hour in court. An
adoption is more than a one-day event in a courtroom—
it's a lifetime of being a family.

Though we aren't a couple anymore, Terry drove down
with us to the adoption. We started the journey of having
a child together, and it felt right to have him with us.

Earlier that week, I had asked Danny what he wanted
to wear to court and he asked for a suit and tie. We went
to the mall to buy him new slacks, a jacket and white shirt.
The dress clothes I bought him in August for my parents'
50th-anniversary cruise were already too small. He asked
me to wear a jacket and tie too. I grew up wearing ties to
church and spent the rest of my youth avoiding wearing
them whenever possible. Danny grew up never wearing
them and tries to put on ties and slacks every chance he
gets. That night, Danny asked if he could sleep with me.

"Why, Danny? It's late and you need to go to bed…"

"I know, Dad, but I don't like being in Tacoma. I'm
scared."

"OK, c'mon over."

"Hurray!" He yelled as he leaped the four-foot span
between the hotel room beds.

"Ouch!" I yelled as he landed on my leg.

"Dad! Are you OK?" Danny is always concerned if anyone around him is hurt.

"Yeah, I'm fine. Try not to do that next time."

"Sorry," he said in a subdued voice.

"How are you feeling?"

"EXCITED!"

"Why?"

"I'm going to be adopted tomorrow! GRRRRRRRR!!!" Danny moved around on the bed making animal sounds. He couldn't contain his excitement. "I wish Rusty were here!"

"Why?"

"Because tomorrow he'll be my brother! RUFF!" He lunged and gave me a play bite. "See, since Rusty isn't here, I can be him!" He started licking my arm and panting.

"Yuck! Quit licking me! Scoot over and let me talk to you," I put my arm around his shoulders. "Do you really believe you're getting adopted?"

"Yes! Terry's here, and he'll be mad at you if you don't adopt me."

"Is that the only reason?"

"No..." The room was quiet, and I could see the moonlight between the cracks of the curtain. "I just know now that it's going to happen."

"Why were you so worried last week?"

"I was afraid you might not like me anymore and you might not want to adopt me."

"I love you, Danny. You are my favorite boy in the world, and I want to create a family with you."

"When I lived with Ms. Benedict, we liked each other for a little while and then she started hating me. I was afraid you might start hating me and get rid of me like she did."

"Have other people wanted to get rid of you, Danny?"

"Yes," he whispered, "they all did. They didn't like me."

"Who didn't like you?"

"My foster homes. My mean grandma."

"You were afraid because your mean grandma and your foster parents didn't want you that I wouldn't want you?"

"Uh-huh."

"Oh..." I didn't speak for a long time. I just held him in the quiet of our dark hotel room. Finally, I broke the silence. "Danny, you made one mistake. Lots of people make it...even adults."

"What?"

"You forgot what a totally great person you are. How could I not adopt a kid as cool as you? You're the best son in the world for me. The only reason those people didn't like you is because they have their own problems. I know you have problems, Dan. So do I. We aren't bad people because of our problems—we're good people because we are trying to grow beyond them. And you've changed. Man oh man, you've grown! I'm so proud of you. I love you so much. And even though I won't like every decision you make, I'll always love you. Always. I promise."

"I love you too, Dad."

"Think you can sleep now?"

"Yep, I am getting tired." He yawned, kissed me good night, and fell asleep his last night as a ward of the state.

Chapter Twenty-Four

Adoption Day

On adoption day morning, the sun was brilliant, the sky was blue, and Mount Rainier rose majestically through the sparse clouds circling its base.

When we arrived at the courthouse, Danny's Aunt Lisa and his twin sisters, Ashley and Emily, were just pulling in. He went running to them and bounced up and down as he kept repeating that he was getting adopted. He was more enthusiastic than an unleashed puppy in a park. While it's unusual to invite birth families to an adoption, Aunt Lisa, Ashley and Emily seemed as excited to be there as Danny was.

When we entered the lobby, his CASA Mike, his case manager Sally, and his social worker Louise all greeted him. His new adoption social worker was unable to attend, and her replacement introduced herself.

"My, this is quite a group," she said. "Who is the lucky kid getting adopted today?" I pointed to Danny. "And you must be the dad?" I nodded. "Where's your wife?" I inwardly rolled my eyes as I explained I was a single parent. The state's incompetence knows no bounds. Here we were at the courthouse, minutes before Danny's adoption, and the state's official representative in court didn't know I was a single parent or who was getting adopted. For a moment, I resented the hundreds of hours I had invested with the state. Just as quickly I dropped it. Changing the system was a battle for another day—today was for Danny and me.

Finally, I saw Franney. My heart leaped and I held back tears. I have known Franney many years, and she had tried to help Terry and me adopt since 2005. She had introduced us to Danny's birthfather, and when Terry and I rejected meeting Danny, she waited. Six months later, she encouraged me again.

"You know I'm only here because of you," I whispered. Franney hugged me, hugged Terry, and we made small talk waiting for the judge. Danny came up to us. A few days before he had written letters to Mike, Sally and Franney to thank them for their part in his adoption.

"Who is Franney again?" he had asked me.

"She's the attorney who introduced me to your birth dad. Without her, I wouldn't have met you."

"Ohhh…"

I was excited to introduce them, "Danny, this is Franney Mack."

"Hi, Danny," Franney held out her hand.

"Actually, he does hug," I offered. Danny grinned and hugged her.

"You are a lucky young man, and I am so glad for you."

"Here, I have something for you," Danny said, shyly handing her an envelope. "Thanks for helping me get adopted."

"You're welcome, Danny."

"I have one for you too," he said as he handed a letter to Mike.

"Is it OK if I read it now?" Mike asked. Danny nodded.

Dear Mike, I am glad that I met Jake. My life hasn't been the same, which is good. What I mean is my life has changed. I haven't got suspended yet and I don't think I will because I have already went half way through the year. I'm going to try my hardest not to get in trouble or get suspended. I can't wait to see you again. Thank you for all the help. Danny

Mike rubbed his eyes and blinked hard. "Thank you, Danny. I'll always treasure this. I am so proud of you." He looked at his watch. "It's time. The judge should be ready for us now."

We followed Mike into the small, oval, modern courtroom. The walls were covered in warm, amber wood with the flags of the United States and Washington State flanking the judge's chair. I have spent many significant moments in courtrooms. Sometimes I was handcuffed, chained and dressed in green coveralls and orange foam slippers. Other times I wore a suit and tie. I have left courtrooms happy, and I have left them sad, but I had never felt this excited to be in court.

As a child, I had always wanted to be a lawyer or judge. I viewed the law as the epitome of justice. It was the final hero standing against bullying, bigotry and evil. I am older now, and I know that courts don't always succeed. The real world isn't like courtrooms on TV. Despite that, I still hold judges, lawyers and the law in high esteem. A society's willingness to apply just laws equally is rooted in our collective aspirations for goodness, kindness, wisdom and equality. I believe that for all their warts and faults, judicial systems have done more to protect, advocate and serve the helpless than any church, legislature or king.

Franney showed us to our seats, and Danny and I sat at the table in front of the judge.

"Are you ready?" I asked Danny. His eyes were bright, and his joy and excitement were as infectious and intense as I'd ever witnessed in another human being.

"I'm ready, Dad." His conviction gave me chills.

"Please rise for the Honorable Kathryn Nelson," the bailiff announced.

"We are here today for a very happy occasion," Judge Nelson said. "Is everyone ready?" There were nods around the room. The judge swore us in and asked a few perfunctory questions for the record. Finally she looked directly at me, "Mr. Dekker, are you willing to adopt Danny to be your son?"

I turned away from her and stared into Danny's eyes. *What should I say? Should I say yes, Danny?* I did my best to keep a twinkle in my eye so he knew I loved him. The courtroom was as quiet as a wedding waiting to hear the bride or groom say, "I do."

Danny met my gaze. *You'd better say yes, Dad. I've put every hope I have on this happening. I love you.*

I turned back to the judge and said loudly, "Yes, your honor. I want Danny to be my son." I turned toward Danny. He was the happiest I'd ever seen him.

"And, Danny, do you want to be adopted by Jake?"

"Yes, I do," his high young voice was solid and firm.

"Before I make my ruling, would anyone like to say anything? Ms. Mack, I see you back there, and I know you're never at a loss for words."

Franney smiled, "Your honor, this is such a happy story. I have known Jake more than 15 years, and I'm honored to be part of this process. I represented Stan, Danny's birth dad, and I can tell the court that this moment is important to him. He knew he couldn't take care of Danny himself, but he wanted to do all he could to make sure his son didn't repeat the same cycle of foster care and jail that he experienced. Also there is an agreement in place for Danny to have contact with his sisters, and they are here in court today. I'm certain that Jake will encourage Danny's relationship with them. I am just happy for both of them."

Danny's CASA, Mike, stood up. "Your honor, I would

like to say something. This is a remarkable story. Danny was a behavioral rehabilitation services kid that we tried to help. Nothing we did really worked. Danny has thrived in Jake's care, and the best thing I can say about this adoption is to look at how well Danny has done in school and at home since he finally received a loving, permanent home. This is what he needed all along—I am so proud and happy for him."

The judge turned back to me. "Mr. Dekker, I have read your home study, the supplements to the home study, the updates to the home study—this has been a long process for you, hasn't it?" She smiled as I nodded in agreement. "And after reviewing them I find you to be a fit and proper parent. I am now signing the decree of adoption. Danny, you are now Danny Dekker, and you are officially adopted."

Danny and I looked dumbly at each other. Franney touched me on the shoulder, "You can hug him now. That was it!" she said in a mock whisper.

I held Danny as my legal son for the first time. His grip was tight. "Why don't you both come up and we'll take a picture," the judge offered.

We walked around the bench, exited the courtroom and entered the podium from the judge's door. *I've never been here before.* The judge almost hugged me, but decorum prevailed and she extended her hand. "Congratulations, Dad," she said loudly, "Thank you, Jake—you're doing a wonderful thing for this child," she whispered for my ears. She turned to Danny. "Would you like to sit in my chair and hold the gavel?"

Terry took our picture. The judge and I are standing side by side, with the flags flanking us, as Danny, the star of the show, held up the gavel to his beaming face. We looked like the cover of an adoption magazine. I thanked the judge, hugged Mike and Terry and finally embraced Franney. "Thanks again," I whispered.

As we left the courtroom, an attorney came up to me. He was sharply dressed and wore a tie with Chinese characters. "Are you Jake Dekker?" He asked.

"Yes..."

"Bob Rickson from Grace International Adoption!"

"Bob, nice to finally meet you." Bob was the director of the adoption agency Terry and I had used when we tried to adopt from Vietnam. We had spoken several times on the phone but never met in person. He was also the attorney Franney suggested we contact when we attempted our first adoption of an infant girl in 2005. He congratulated me, and I introduced him to Terry.

How strange. I feel like Dorothy waking up in Kansas after her journey to Oz and seeing the Scarecrow, Tin Man, and Cowardly Lion in the faces of the farmhands. Everything was coming full circle.

Danny left for a short trip to get breakfast with his sisters. Terry, Franney and I waited to get copies of the adoption decree and then went for coffee. It felt complete that the adoption morning ended with Terry, Franney and me. When Danny returned, we said good-bye to Franney and Terry. Soon it was just Danny and me in the car, alone for the first time as legal father and son.

"How are you feeling, Dan?"

"GREAT! This was the best day of my life!"

"What was your favorite moment?"

He paused to consider it. "When we were at the table and the judge said 'You are adopted' and then I hugged you."

"That might be my favorite moment too—I also liked it when the judge called me a fit and proper parent. Sometimes when I was in court before today the judge said other things about me that were true—but they weren't always nice."

"Yeah, I know. You told me you went to jail before. How long were you there?"

"I made some bad decisions, Danny, and I was there too long. We'll talk about it another day. I just feel really happy that the judge made us a family. Are you ready to visit your old school?" I had arranged for Danny to see his former fourth-grade teacher. She was excited to see him and arranged her schedule to spend a half hour with us. From the time I contacted her about the possibility of visiting, she had sent me four emails. As we approached the school, I asked Danny how it felt to be going back there.

"Good, 'cuz now I'm adopted." We parked, and he ran around showing me places he used to hide and the rocks and retaining walls he used to jump over.

"See, Dad! That's where I waited for the bus—until I got kicked off and had to take the short bus." He pointed to the front of the school. We walked in, and Danny immediately headed to Mrs. Reynolds' room.

"Danny! Wait! We have to check in at the office." He led the way—he knew the school as well as the woods around our house.

"My, you look good, Danny!" the secretary said as she handed him his visitor badge. "We've been expecting you. We heard about what happened today. Congratulations on being adopted." Danny beamed from her compliments as he triumphantly left the office he'd been sent to so often for getting in trouble.

Danny didn't know that some of the staff at his old school had wanted to move him to a self-contained class-room. His behavior was too disruptive, and some staff were willing to sacrifice a "thrownaway" foster kid to create a better learning environment for his classmates. Mrs. Reynolds fought for him to stay in her class. She re-peatedly stated in meetings, conferences and emails that Danny was a young man worth saving.

She knew Danny had a horrific background. Even though Mrs. Reynolds must have known it was unlikely that a legally free special-needs child Danny's age would be adopted, something made her fight for him. Mrs. Reynolds was seated at her desk as we walked in. Danny went running to her.

"Hi, Mrs. Reynolds!" He hugged her tightly. "Guess what? I'm adopted!"

"I know. That is so exciting, Danny. It is good to see you! I am happy for you—you look so healthy. I always worried about how thin you were." She looked at me in disbelief. I asked for directions to the restroom so they had a chance to visit privately. A few minutes later, I returned.

"Mrs. Reynolds, may I please go next door to take a picture of the snails?" Danny asked.

"Sure, honey, you go right ahead."

Mrs. Reynolds looked at me. Before she could speak, tears filled her eyes. "You have no idea how much I worried about that child. I knew there was a good kid in there somewhere, but it was hard to find. Do you know anything about his foster mother, Ms. Benedict? I was always suspicious of her. I have had other kids in my class that lived with her, and none of them ever seemed happy. I don't think she treated him well."

"Yes, I do know about her. Your instincts were correct. She didn't treat him well. I know we don't have much time before Danny comes back, so I need to tell you how much I appreciate your fighting for him to stay in your classroom. I know you really went to bat for him, and I wanted you to see how much your effort paid off. He's doing really well now. He turns in a lot of his homework, he's reading close to grade level—even his math is improving. But most important, he's happy."

"I always knew he could do it," she said. "He just needed

somebody to love him, somebody to care for him. He has such a sweet spirit. It amazed me that he could keep that sweetness and kindness about him after everything he's gone through. I need to tell you, you're an angel. You're his angel, and you are my angel."

I tried to reply, but for the first time on adoption day my emotions rendered me speechless. I loved this woman, this teacher of children who fought for my son. We played on the same team even though today was the first day we'd met. "Thank you," I finally said. "He's a great kid, and I love him."

Danny returned, and we said our good-byes. Mrs. Reynolds gave me her home phone number and made me promise to keep in touch.

"Danny, when you graduate from high school you have to send me an invitation. I am going to come and watch you graduate. Listen to your dad. I am proud of you—I always knew you could do it."

Danny beamed. He was the conquering hero returning home for a visit, but he was also the child learning you can't go home again; it changes while you're away.

"I will, Mrs. Reynolds. Thank you. I love you."

"Bye, Danny. I love you too." She turned to me, "I never thought I would see him looking this healthy and happy."

As we left the school parking lot, Danny asked, "Dad, may we drive by Ms. Benedict's house?"

"I don't know, Danny. This is a happy day. Are you sure that's something you want to do today?"

"Yep. I want to see the house and laugh at it, and if she takes her big 400-pound butt out the door to yell at me I'm going to say 'you can't do nuthin' to me 'cuz I'm adopted now,' OK?"

"OK, it's your day. Tell me how to get there." He directed me through the neighborhood he knew so well. As we approached his old foster home, he tensed up. He banished his fear with bold laughter.

"Look, Dad. That's where she fell down!" I was proud of his courage. Proud that he was facing his demons. He made me drive by her house twice, and then we headed home.

"You know, you're my son now—"

"And you're my dad—"

"Does it feel different now, Dan?"

"Yeah, a little."

"Do you believe I am going to adopt you now?"

"Yes, because you did!"

A few hours later we arrived home. We dropped by his school to give them a copy of the adoption decree so they could officially change his last name on their records. His principal came out to greet us. "You sure look happy today, Danny," she said with a twinkle in her eye.

"That's 'cuz I'm adopted now," He was still beaming from ear to ear.

"I know. Congratulations, Danny. We're all proud of you and happy for you and your dad." He smiled at her, and we went home.

As we pulled in the driveway, Danny said, "Stop, Dad! Let me out!" Danny ran into the house shouting, "Rusty! Rusty!" Rusty dashed out and jumped on his chest. "Hi, brother! We're home, and you're my brother now 'cuz I'm adopted! C'mon, Rusty. Chase me! Chase me!" Danny ran as Rusty chased him, both lost in the timeless joy of a boy and his dog leaping and playing together in the home they will always share.

Chapter Twenty-Five

A New Life

When I woke up the next morning, I saw the stack of adoption papers on my dresser. *I really did it. I'm Danny's dad now. I am responsible for a kid!* The weight of it hit me. I hadn't considered not adopting him since I decided to make him my son. But now that it had happened, I couldn't help reflecting on what I had done. *Am I ready for this? Can I do a good enough job?* As my doubts and fears threatened to overwhelm me, a fierce clarity whispered: *You are as ready as you need to be. No one is ever completely ready to be a parent. You'll learn as you go, and when you need help it will always be there. Be happy. You made a wise choice. Love him and enjoy your new life.*

The next day I invited a bunch of our friends to celebrate Danny's adoption. We met in a small room at a pizza parlor. It was packed with about 35 people. I had asked Bill and Barbara to make a few remarks. Bill is my 12-Step sponsor; Barbara was my counselor. Both have known me more than 20 years. They have watched my progression from a dysfunctional, immature, self-centered young adult to the man I am today.

Although I had asked for no gifts, a few came anyway. The most extraordinary was a book of memories and photos that a friend had put together for Danny. On the second page she had created a "family tree of a different kind." At the bottom was Danny, his sisters and me, but she included branches for all the members of the "family" raising Danny.

When everyone finished eating, Danny stood up to read me a letter. As the room grew quiet, he adjusted his feet, scratched his nose, shifted uncomfortably and finally began.

"Dear Dad, I hope you like this letter. If you don't, well then, I'll have to do a new letter. The first day I came to live with you I was kind of scared. But after a while I got used to Anacortes. I got in trouble a few times and said I couldn't change. But look, seven months later I don't get in trouble anymore and I've changed a lot. But just two days ago the best day of my life happened. I got adopted by guess who? You! I will bless that day forever and I will always be your son. Love, your son. Danny Dekker."

After the clapping finished, my sponsor, Bill, got up, "I'd like to share some of my thoughts and memories about this beautiful union. First, I'd like to share Christmas Eve. That's really the first time the impact of Jake and Danny hit me. Our front door burst open and here was this little guy running in. He went right up to my wife, hugged her, and said 'Merry Christmas. You mean so much to me.'

"There was an incident last summer that says a lot about both of them. Jake had come up to our house, and I watched him unloading a bicycle from his truck that Danny had put there. Jake wasn't happy about it. There's a little more to this than I'm getting into right now—"

"I told Danny he couldn't put the bike in the truck!" I interrupted. Several people laughed.

"That's right. You told him he couldn't take it. I watched Danny get on his bicycle, and there was a tense moment because Danny wanted to ride home. It was twilight, almost dark. And I watched Jake just surrender to him. He turned on his car's headlights and said, 'Let me follow you and light the way home.' And that to me portends exactly where they're going. Jake's preparation for adopting Danny has been long and arduous. I know because I have been there every step of the way. May God's grace bless this union. May His will be done."

Everyone clapped as Bill sat down and Barbara got up to speak. "I've tried to figure out what I'm going to say about a man I've known since 1989. When I first met Jake, he was in the throes of an incredible spiritual depression. He was totally lost and completely ruled by his ego. He tried to look good at any cost. And then I got to be part of his unfolding through 12-Step recovery programs and personal development. I knew Jake had a big heart; Bill knew Jake had a big heart. I don't think we would have hung in there if we didn't see that.

"All along, Jake was making these extended family connections. That is spiritual intelligence. I think of Jake's life a little like the *Odyssey*, always trying to get home to his family. That was the way Jake's life was for many years. Going through all these different adventures, all these different obstacles, going over them, going through them, but never going around them.

"When Jake's life looked as if it was the easiest it could possibly be, he turned the boat and sailed right into the biggest wave by taking Danny. That's the sign of somebody whose personal growth is the most important thing. He recognized there is something deeper and truer."

Barbara turned to me. "Because of your ability, intelligence, big heart and your willingness to reach out to all the people in this room, you have received the love and support you needed for you and Danny. The miracle is we are all better for it. That's the beauty of this. We are better for it, and Danny has a circle of protection, love and connection all around him.

"Jake has taught me. He has given me some of the most wonderful moments of my life. Who are the teachers and who are the students? There comes a time when the teacher sits at the foot of the student and says, 'Please teach me, because now you are the teacher.'"

It was hard to hear all the things Bill and Barbara said. But they are true. I have grown, and somewhere along the way I acquired the ability to give Danny the love, stability, care, protection and home he needs.

This is the end of the adoption journey, but the beginning of our life journey together. For the rest of our lives and memories, I am Danny's dad and he is my son. I don't know how our lives will unfold. I know that the time between now and when Danny leaves home won't always be easy. I was telling my brother about some of my fears and he said, "Look out. Middle school is coming. You can expect a lot of adult-style issues without the benefit of mature judgment."

I believe that with support, encouragement, experience, and most of all love, I can be a good parent. The only limits are my fear and insecurity. Danny has seen a therapist ever since he moved in with me. Last week she said, "I wish we had a before and after picture—not just all of the physical things. Danny just isn't the same kid."

Everyone who has watched us—his teachers, therapists, friends and family—have seen a miracle unfold. It makes me wonder. Is it a miracle? Certainly it's out of the ordinary. Troubled foster children don't usually change this quickly. But how many other kids in foster homes who hate their lives, feel worthless, abandoned and unloved could experience the same miracle as Danny if given an opportunity? Is it possible that every kid can achieve a miracle if angels appear? Maybe the angels are already here. Maybe the angels are us.

Life is short. I can't change the world, but I intend to use the resources and abilities I have to help Danny and other kids like him. There are many good causes in the world—alleviating extreme poverty, Special Olympics, recovery from addiction, fighting cancer, and feeding the hungry all spring to mind—but creating authentic attachment for children is my passion. With good health, and a little luck I can spend the rest of my life doing that. Jesus taught in the parable of the lost sheep that the key to the many is the one, and I believe the secret to bringing hope, community and attachment to neglected "thrown-away" kids is to love and help them—one kid at a time.

Chapter Twenty-Six

Eighteen Months Later

"Don't let anybody see you, Dad!" Danny pleaded from the passenger seat. It was seven a.m., and he was boarding the school bus for his first day of middle school. I had dreaded this day since Danny's adoption. Part of it was my concern for my 12-year-old son's initiation into the purgatory between elementary and high school known as middle school or junior high, but a lot of it was my distaste for getting up early.

My natural rhythm seems to be to fall asleep around midnight and get up around eight. In elementary school we got up at 8:30. Today, and for the next six years, I have to get up at six on school days. To make the best of it, I put on gym clothes and rode my exercise bike for 20 minutes, as Danny got ready for school. After I made him breakfast (that's what I call pouring cereal in a bowl and throwing some vitamins on the table), I needed something to fill the time between waking him up and driving him to his bus stop. Going back to bed seemed cruel to Danny, and ever since he had a school lesson on the dangers of obesity and the related risk of heart attack, he has encouraged me to get exercise and lose weight.

His bus takes 45 minutes to travel a distance that takes 15 minutes to drive. Three years ago, Danny was permanently expelled from the school bus. I knew that riding a bus again might be a trigger for him, so I drove him to elementary school every morning.

"Why do you care if anyone sees me, Danny?"

"It's embarrassing, Dad!" he looked exasperated. "I don't want other kids to see me waiting with you!"

"Why? I thought you were proud of me. Don't you still think I'm a good dad?" I tried to look hurt but I was smiling inside—proud of him for wanting independence.

"You're a good dad, but I'm not a little kid anymore... I want to do it myself." I didn't say anything. A few moments later he said, "I love you, Dad," as he squeezed my hand.

"I love you too, Danny. Why don't I drop you off at the end of the road and I'll park behind the trees to make sure you get picked up, OK?"

"Sure!" he grinned at me. "That's perfect. Thanks, Dad!" He grabbed his new school bag that our friend got him with his name stenciled on it, his cross-country clothes and shoes inside, and he slammed the car door. "Bye! Love you!" I felt great.

He seemed as ready as anyone is to enter middle school, and I had done everything I knew to help him make a smooth transition. He had ended weekly therapy months ago—he and his therapist decided he didn't need to come in as often—and he has successfully stayed off all psychotropic medications for almost two years.

The bus came, and Danny was gone. The sun was rising over Mount Baker, and I decided that I needed to follow the bus. Just this one day I wanted to see where Danny went every morning and how long it took to get to school. I did my best to make sure that Danny didn't witness his hyper-vigilant father stalking him to school. I watched him get off the bus—he seemed small compared with the other kids he rode with—and I went home to get ready for work. The first day of class was also his first day of cross-country practice. He ran several miles and couldn't wait to tell me about it.

Last year my friend who teaches at Danny's school told me Danny needed to take band as an elective. The band teacher works with students from the seventh through twelfth grades. His love of music, skill with students and ability to educate and inspire with songs is priceless. Teachers like him inspired the movie *Mr. Holland's Opus*. Danny wanted to play drums in the band, but most other boys wanted that too. Knowing he probably wouldn't be selected for drums, Danny requested the trombone. A few days later the band director confirmed him as a middle school trombonist.

Because I'm a single parent, work full time and have too

many worthwhile commitments, I often feel short of time. I love having a son, and I know I was meant to be Danny's dad, but some days with him are easier than others. On Wednesday when I got home, Danny had bad news. "Dad, I was suspended from cross-country tomorrow."

Danny likes to tease—he gets it from me—and I wasn't in the mood. "Danny, I don't have time for that right now. You love cross-country, and you weren't suspended. C'mon, we need to get dinner."

"No, really!" he protested. "I was suspended from cross-country for a day!" He looked upset, and I realized he was telling the truth.

"Really?" He nodded. I felt anger toward him along with anxiety about what to do tomorrow after school. Cross-country practice lasts till 4:30, but school ends at 2:30. Before school started, I told Danny he had to pick soccer, football or cross-country after school, as coming home to an empty house isn't an option. The economy is too poor and money is too tight for me to leave work every day at 2 p.m. "What happened, Danny?" I asked.

"Well, I was running," he stammered, "and I was tired, so I started walking and there were these eighth-graders with me, and then the coach told us to run and they started saying 'Why don't you start running' to her, then they laughed at her and then I said some stuff too…" he looked up at me anxiously. "And then she got really mad and told us we couldn't come to cross-country tomorrow because we were suspended for a day for being bad."

"Let me see if I have this right. You weren't running at practice and you were sassy to your cross-country coach?"

"Yeah, I'm really sorry, Dad. I didn't say most of the bad things, but I did say a few things… I'm really sorry," he looked despondent. His eyes wouldn't meet mine.

"Tomorrow you need to write your coach a note apologizing, and I'll figure out what else needs to happen." I wrote his coach an email sharing some of Danny's background. She explained that Danny wasn't the ringleader. Unfortunately, he struggles with impulsivity and always seems to get caught.

As it turned out, the two other boys were permanently expelled from the team two days later after calling the coach a bitch. Fortunately, Danny wasn't anywhere near them when it happened.

Today we got Danny's trombone. We rented-to-own a beautiful, slightly used instrument. "Look how shiny it is, Dad!" he said as he pulled it out of the case. "The mouthpiece is real silver. Isn't it heavy?" His eyes glowed with pride as he handed it to me.

"Do you want to try to play it?"

"Yes!" he nodded, and for a moment I caught a flash of the ten-year-old hyper, impulsive Danny. He placed the mouthpiece into the horn and blew. WAH-WAH! WAH-WAH! It was loud! An irrepressible grin formed as he pulled the mouthpiece away from his lips. "I love this, Dad."

"Tell you what. You blow that pretty well. Let's stop by grandpa and grandma's house, sneak in and surprise them with your horn." He flashed a devilish grin and nodded.

We pulled in to my parents' driveway, and I quietly opened the front door. My 78-year-old father spotted us from the couch, but my mom was asleep in a chair. I nodded to Danny. WAH-WAH! WAH-WAH! filled their living room as he blew loudly while moving the trombone's slide. My mother jerked awake and yelled, "OOH! WHAT? WHAT! What's that?" It took her a moment to realize Danny was a few feet away from the couch blowing into a trombone.

Because she's generally good-natured, she laughed at the incongruity of being awakened by a trombone in her living room. My dad and I thought it was funny too. On the way home, I let Danny play the trombone as the car passed unsuspecting strangers. Most of them seemed amused, but a few gave us dirty looks. It was impossible for me to hear the joy and passion in Danny's notes without getting caught up in his enthusiasm.

"This is fun, Dad," Danny giggled. "I love the trombone." I don't know if his excitement for the trombone, riding the school bus or attending middle school will last, but for now he loves his instrument, he can't wait to see Dave, "his" bus driver and sit with other kids on the way to school. He thinks leaving elementary school and going to middle school is "really cool."

The first day of middle school is an initiation I wouldn't

choose to experience again, but it feels right to be supporting Danny. And that has been our story—it feels right to be supporting Danny.

When I chose to let a scared, anxious, neglected, diagnosed-with-damn-near-every-psychological-disorder-you-wouldn't-want-your-kid-to-have ten-year-old boy come live with me in hopes of adopting him, my head told me this was the craziest decision I'd ever considered. But my heart sang this was the wisest choice I'd ever make. And though I lost some of my day-to-day tranquility, I traded it for a life filled with meaning, uncertainty and love.

Regardless of what the future holds, none of us know how our children's lives will unfold. No matter what happens from here, I've had a ringside seat to a miracle, and as much as Danny has grown, I've grown at least that much too.

CHAPTER TWENTY-SEVEN

THREE YEARS LATER

Three years after Danny moved in, our 11-year-old dog, Rusty, neared the end of his life. Rusty's health problems made it painfully obvious that the family the three of us had created would change with his passing.

When Danny arrived from foster care, he was frightened, skittish, anxious and scared. From the first night he spent with me, he insisted Rusty sleep with him. He wouldn't go upstairs without having Rusty go with him. That lasted almost two years.

My own relationship with Rusty suffered when Danny joined us. Our duo became a trio, and Danny needed Rusty more than I did. Rusty knew it. He never resented leaving my room and sleeping with Danny instead. When Danny yelled at him to follow him upstairs, the most Rusty balked was to look at me as if to ask, "Must I?" Danny is 13 now. His fears are typical of a 13-year-old, and he no longer requires Rusty to feel secure.

A little over a year ago, Rusty started limping. He

was diagnosed with degenerative myelopathy, which means that through irreversible nerve damage he would eventually lose all control of his back legs, bowels, urine and front paws. The vet who diagnosed him wanted to do surgery but I refused when I learned the surgery could only confirm the diagnosis. There is no cure. By November, Rusty could only drag his body with his front paws, so I bought him a dog wheelchair.

I could see Rusty was deteriorating, but his quality of life seemed high and the thought of putting him down was too horrific for Danny or me to consider. A few weeks ago, Rusty started noticeably withdrawing from life. He didn't try to get up when people approached him, and he sometimes didn't move for many hours at a time. Earlier this week, the nerve damage finally spread to his bladder. He peed all over the house, in the office, in the car and in the garage. My only option was to buy diapers or move him outside. I knew it was time. Many things are beyond my ability to control, and death and mortality are at the top of that list.

In a few days, Danny was leaving on a three-week rite-of-passage journey for boys during which he would hike 60 miles in the Olympic rainforest, spend 24 hours alone without food on a beach, and participate in a program intended to help him with his passage from childhood to becoming a young man. It seemed cruel to keep Rusty alive till Danny returned home, and Danny insisted on being home when Rusty died.

The day before his death, Danny and I played with Rusty. I shed many tears but Danny acted numb. I worried about how Rusty's imminent death was affecting him—he didn't show much emotion but I knew he was hurting inside. That afternoon, we dug a large grave in our front lawn and arranged for a vet to come to our house the next day, sedate Rusty and then stop his heart.

"What are you going to miss most about Rusty when he's gone?" I asked Danny as we drove to dig Rusty's grave at our house in the woods.

Without hesitating he replied, "Him. Him, Dad. I'm just going to miss him."

"Me too."

On the day of Rusty's death, it was hard to get out of bed. Some days are difficult to face. I wanted to be alone, or be with just Danny when Rusty was put down, but the night before as my dad was on the floor saying good-bye to Rusty he asked to be there. "What time should we come over?" my dad asked.

"Around 7 or 7:30. I'll have some pizza and salad so you don't need to eat. We also need to say good-bye to Danny before his trip."

"No, what time is the vet coming." My mother caught my eye and looked at me anxiously.

"At 5, Dad. She's coming at 5."

"I think I need to be there," he said slowly. My 79-year-old dad's speech is thick from having Parkinson's, and he struggles to find words because of his Alzheimer's.

"Honey," my mom said, "you don't really want to be there when Rusty is put down, do you?"

He slowly turned his eyes toward her and softly said, "Yes. I think I do." My mom looked at me helplessly.

"Dad, I really don't want anyone but Danny and me there. I've asked Terry to come so he can be in the house if it's too hard for Danny, though I kind of wanted to be alone. But if you're sure you need to be there, then I guess you can come over."

"I think I do."

"OK. We'll work it out." Rarely have I heard my father have so much clarity.

The morning of his death, Rusty came over to me in his wheelchair. He sniffed me and licked me for a good 15 minutes. I tried to push him away, but he just kept placing his muzzle under my hand. He has never licked me so long before. Rusty has acted differently toward Danny and me the past few days. His demeanor has been youthful, he seems happy, and he has enjoyed being with everyone. I started crying as I realized it felt as if Rusty were trying to remember my scent and my taste so some day, when we are in another Great Mystery together, he can find and recognize me again.

Around noon, Danny and I drove Rusty from our beach cabin to the house in the woods where he will be buried. Danny distracted himself by chopping wood and riding his bike. I distracted myself by putting cushions in the outdoor chairs, creating natural alters circling the space I prepared for the vet and Rusty outside, and placing photos, candles and memories of Rusty on the dining room table.

When the vet finally arrived, I carried Rusty one last time to the space I created on the lawn. Old trees, ferns, birds, grass and the woods surrounded us. The sun was dimly out, and it was cool but not uncomfortably cold. I laid Rusty on the receiving blanket my mother brought me home in when I was born. It seemed appropriate that Rusty leave this world wrapped by the blanket I had arrived in. Because it was too small for him, I also placed a gray British Air first-class blanket from my dad around him. I liked the idea of Rusty's traveling first class on his final journey.

The vet sedated him, and within minutes Rusty was still and calm. I held and supported his head with my two hands, stroked him and said all the things I could think of to let him know that I would be with him till the end. I told him the fight was over—he was a valiant warrior—but now it was time to let go and be free.

Danny was sitting about 20 feet away at the table, flinching and nervous from the vet poking Rusty with needles. "Can I come over, Dad?"

"Of course you can. Come on over, Dan." He joined me, and we both sat cross-legged on the lawn, petting Rusty and telling him how much we loved him. I don't know what Danny and I would have done without Rusty. His contribution to the creation of our family is immeasurable and unique.

The vet had a hard time. Because of Rusty's disease, his veins were almost impossible to find. She spent more than 25 minutes poking him, trying to hit a vein. Rusty didn't react to any of the pokes of her needles.

"Thank God!" The vet blurted out. She looked away embarrassed, "Sorry, I've just never taken this long to find a vein. Rusty is the all-time marathon winner."

"It's fine," I replied. As soon as I saw Rusty's blood in the catheter tube I knew she finally succeeded. The blood upset Danny. I forgot that many people don't know that when you hit a vein, blood backfills through the needle. The sight of blood still makes Danny squeamish.

"I'm going to start now," the vet said. I looked Rusty in the eyes and whispered everything intuitive and sacred I knew to say to him, as Danny caressed him, listened and watched.

"I think we both need to be touching him when he dies, Dad." I nodded to Danny and stroked Rusty as my tears fell on his fur. Danny kept one hand on Rusty's back and the other scratched his ears. As I kept looking in Rusty's eyes, I suddenly knew our doggie was gone. I didn't feel the shift, he didn't move or flinch, and there was no sound. But his eyes felt different. Though they would have looked the same to a camera, I knew that his soul had departed. Eyes are the windows of the soul.

"I think he's gone," I told the vet. She pulled out her stethoscope and listened. She nodded. It was done.

Danny and I stood up together, and I hugged him. Danny has cried in my arms many times, but this time the tears in our embrace were mine. I wrapped Rusty tightly in the blankets and lifted him to the back of the John Deere trailer that Danny had attached to the lawnmower he had commandeered as a hearse to take Rusty from the backyard to the front. I held my warm, lifeless dog as I have held him every morning for the past eight months as I carried him down the stairs he could no longer climb. I knew he was gone. Dead bodies feel different than live ones.

Danny drove Rusty to the front yard. We lifted his limp body out together and gently placed him in his grave and spread dried roses over him. My father offered a prayer. Then we shoveled the dirt and replaced the grass.

"Wait, Dad! Wait!" Danny had carved a piece of wood as a grave marker. He placed two hearts on either side of "R.I.P. RUSTY." He carefully positioned the marker on the grass that now covered Rusty's body.

"Thank you, Danny. Rusty will like that. It's beautiful. You did a good job."

We spent an hour with my parents and a few close friends before driving to the beach cabin in the dark. On the drive home, Danny looked at me. "Dad?"

"Yes?"

"Dad..." his voice cracked, "I'm really going to miss

him…" He started sobbing. "I'm going to miss him so much!" I hadn't seen Danny cry yet. I was relieved to see him sobbing. He has seen many tears from me this week. I've told him that Rusty deserves my tears—that grief is praise for the departed—and that strength and courage from being a man doesn't come from suppressing my grief, it comes from feeling the sadness and honoring the departed by releasing it. It is easier for me to suppress grief than express it, but my relationship to my dog is too sacred to resort to old defenses that never served me well anyway.

"It's OK, buddy. It's OK. I miss him too. Do you know what we have to do now?"

"Take care of each other?" he said through his tears and runny nose.

"Yes, that too. But I was thinking of your new cat, Taz. This is sad, and we will both always miss Rusty. But Taz needs us now too."

"He'll be sad, won't he?"

"Yes. He will. When you're away, I'll even let him stay in my room." Danny knows I don't like sleeping with his new cat. "Do you know what happened to me this morning, Danny?" The moonlight reflected on the farmland as the distance between Rusty's grave and our car grew. "I was in the shower, and I started crying. I cried really hard. I even moaned. I like crying in the shower, Danny, because people can't hear me there. It's a good place to cry." Danny smiled at me through his pain. "Anyway, I was crying hard and all I could think to do was ask my grandma to help

Rusty. I kept saying 'Please take care of my doggie. Please, please take care of my doggie.' And do you know what? I think she will. I think all my grandpas, my grandmas, Terry's mom, my Uncle Jake and all my other loved ones will be there for Rusty.

"You see, Danny, I don't believe that death ends a relationship. I can't tell you why I feel that, I can't prove it to you, and you will need to discover your own truth about what you believe for yourself. But in some ways I feel as close to my grandma, and she feels as real to me today, as she did when she was alive. I hope you remember that. Someday I'll probably be gone and you'll be living here without me and you'll miss me. I want you to know that I believe death doesn't end relationships. They change, sure, but they go on, and Rusty, like my grandma, and you will always be with me. It just won't be the same, and because of that I'm very sad."

I didn't sleep well that night. Danny crawled in bed with me and was squirming around. The cat jumped up and down at least a dozen times, and the pizza I ate gave me heartburn. About 3:30, I woke up from a deep dream. I looked down at the side of my bed, and Rusty was lying on the floor! I knew he was dead, but there he was. I blinked a few times and slowly his form drifted into my pillow that had fallen to the carpet. I lost it. I couldn't stop crying, so I left my bedroom, went out to the deck and listened to the ocean lapping under the cool Pacific Northwest starry sky as I mourned the loss of our dog.

This will be hard. But it is also a time for great gratitude.

Our lives would be immeasurably worse without Rusty. I might not have adopted Danny if I hadn't successfully raised a dog. When Danny came into my life a friend wrote, "If you do as good a job with Danny as you've done with Rusty, you will be an amazing father." I've tried. Rusty was easier. He minded better. He was a true gentleman. Danny is a fledgling teenager. He is a human. He is complex, and he forces me to face my own issues.

Life is a short pause between two great mysteries. My heart knows no limit to my gratitude for sharing that brief time with Rusty and Danny. I expect the three of us and our loved ones will be together again in the mysteries that bookend birth and death. My relationship with Rusty and Danny feels as deep, intense and sacred as any I've experienced. In the same way music touches the soul, love can bypass ego, jealousy, competition and fear and simply connect us. The only thing greater than my feeling of loss is my gratitude for our time together.

Rest in peace, Rusty. Godspeed and all good wishes till we meet again. And meeting again, for those who love each other, is inevitable.

IMPROVING THE SYSTEM

What do we teach our children in school? We teach them that two and two are four and that Paris is the capital of France. When will we also teach them what they are? We should say to each of them: Do you know what you are? You are a marvel. You are unique. In all the world there is no other child exactly like you. In the millions of years that have passed, there has never been a child like you. And look at your body—what a wonder it is! Your legs, your arms, your cunning fingers, the way you move! You may become a Shakespeare, a Michelangelo, a Beethoven. You have the capacity for anything. Yes, you are a marvel. And when you grow up, can you harm another who is, like you, a marvel? You must cherish one another. We must all work to make this world worthy of its children.
                                                        —Pablo Casals

Many well-meaning people have tried to repair the child-welfare system. Although almost everyone involved with it agrees it is broken, there is no consensus on how to fix it.

Jim Casey, the founder of United Parcel Service, and his family made an unprecedented effort to improve the system. He and his siblings established the Annie E. Casey Foundation, worth over $2.8 billion,[9] to help disadvantaged children through research, advocacy and direct services to foster children.

Despite the efforts and resources of the Casey Foundation, government social service agencies, conscientious lawmakers and numerous child-welfare advocates, the child-welfare system continues to produce abysmal results for children. Consider the following:

◆ Approximately 424,000 U.S. children were in foster care in 2009[10]. The majority are victims of abuse or neglect.

◆ The U.S. child-welfare system spends over $25 billion dollars annually to provide services for children[11].

◆ Approximately 29,500 children turn 18 and "age out" of foster care in the United States every year[12].

◆ Many children are worse off in foster care than in the troubled homes they were removed from [13].

◆ Former foster youth are one-third as likely to have a high school diploma or GED, half as likely to have attended any college and one-fifth as likely to have a college degree as children who never experienced foster care[14].

◆ Former foster youth males are three times as likely to be convicted of a crime after turning 18. Females are nine times as likely to be convicted of a crime than children who never experienced foster care[15].

✦ Former foster youth are three times more likely to be unable to pay their rent and are at much greater risk of homelessness[16] than children who never experienced foster care.

✦ It is estimated that more than 70% of the U.S. prison population are former foster kids [17].

✦ Foster children are 2.7 to 4.5 times more likely to be prescribed expensive Medicaid-provided psychotropic drugs, and thousands of foster children, including some younger than one year old, are taking daily doses that are higher than the maximum safe level recognized by the FDA[18].

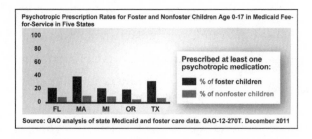

Psychotropic Prescription Rates for Foster and Nonfoster Children Age 0-17 in Medicaid Fee-for-Service in Five States

Prescribed at least one psychotropic medication:
■ % of foster children
□ % of nonfoster children

Source: GAO analysis of state Medicaid and foster care data. GAO-12-270T. December 2011

In the United States it is estimated that 5% of all children are prescribed psychotropic medication.[19] This is one of the highest percentages for medicating children of any country in the world. The percentage of foster children taking psychotropic medication in the United States is much greater. Experts estimate that anywhere from 13% to 52%[20] of foster children are forced to take drugs, and foster children are 2.7 to 4.5 times more likely to be prescribed expensive Medicaid-provided psychotropic drugs than children who aren't in foster care.[21]

While some children certainly benefit from taking psychotropic medication, it is obvious that foster children as a group are significantly overmedicated.

To make a serious dent in the prison, homeless and welfare populations, we must find a way to nurture and love these "thrownaway" kids. Despite spending more than $500 million dollars[22] annually on child-welfare services in Washington State alone, the system is broken. Kids turn 18 and are basically told, "Have a nice life." There are no real support systems to help them.

Legislation intended to allow kids to remain in foster care until age 21 helps only the most responsible, disciplined teenagers. The majority of foster kids don't have the maturity to stay out of trouble and can be thrown out of care if they break the rules[23] after turning 18. Many have no home to return to for the holidays, no one to call if they get an A on an exam, go on a date, end a relationship, get pregnant, jailed, injured, married, promoted or fired.

When foster kids turn 18 and "age out" of the child-welfare system, they often end up "couch surfing," struggling to keep "McJobs", moving to homeless shelters, getting arrested, getting pregnant, going on welfare and serving time in jail. Many never graduate from high school and are far less likely to attend or graduate from college[24].

The Chapin Hill Center for Children at the University

of Chicago undertook a pioneering study of children aging out of foster care. They started following 723 young adults who were 17 or 18 years old and still in foster care, to learn what would happen to them as they transitioned into adulthood and had to live on their own. The following two quotes from their research summarizes the challenges of former foster children:

> "*In comparison to their peers, these young adults [former foster children] are on average less likely to have a high school diploma, less likely to be pursuing higher education, less likely to be earning a living wage, more likely to have experienced economic hardships, more likely to have had a child outside of wedlock and more likely to have become involved with the criminal justice system[25].*"

> "*The picture that emerges from data we collected when they were 23 and 24 years old is disquieting, particularly if we measure their success in terms of self-sufficiency. Across a wide range of outcome measures, including postsecondary educational attainment, employment, housing stability, public assistance receipt and criminal justice system involvement, these former foster youth are faring poorly as a group both in an absolute sense and relative to young adults in the general population.*" ... "*...far too many foster youth are not acquiring the life skills or developing the interpersonal connections they*

will need if they are to become productive young adults[26]."

The financial and human resources that society puts toward helping foster children are immense. Simple arithmetic reveals that dividing the $25 billion in federal and state tax dollars spent annually by the approximately 424,000 foster children in care, results in an average of $58,962 in child-welfare system funding annually per child.

Although not every dollar in child-welfare services is spent on foster children and related services, the majority of the dollars are. What are we getting for our money? Abysmal outcomes, and despite regular efforts to reform the system, the "same old same old" as we try to improve results using outdated practices, tools and resources proven time and again to fail.

Albert Einstein is famously quoted as saying the significant problems we face cannot be solved at the same level of thinking we were at when we created them. Psychologist Carl Jung observed that the greatest and most important problems of life are all fundamentally insoluble. They can never be solved but only outgrown.

How do we "outgrow" the problems the child-welfare system was created to address? How do we find innovative, inspired, sensible solutions for abandoned, neglected and abused children?

Any authentic change to the foster-care system must be a co-creative effort by a wide variety of stakeholders. We need economists, social workers, psychologists, parents, politicians, teachers, foster parents, medical experts, religious leaders, government workers and current and former foster children. A diverse community needs to contribute ideas, find points of consensus and be willing to consider and propose new (and sometimes unpopular) ways of helping children.

The system can't change itself; it is too invested in its own existence. Bureaucracies often lose sight of why they were established and become focused on their own survival and desire for self-preservation. For example, the child-welfare system pays most foster parents very little for taking care of children and has a small budget for direct services such as tutors, counselors, sports equipment, clothing, braces, toys, school supplies, toiletries, snacks, books, musical instruments, tennis shoes and extra-curricular school activities, compared with how much they spend on salaries, overhead and bureaucratic expenses.

True reform must originate from outside the child-welfare system, as most of the employees entrenched there are incapable of proposing innovative approaches that might result in the loss of their jobs and the demise of the system they know.

A better system must rely on the principle that society has the power to create attachment for children. Until our efforts are based on this, the idea that we are genuinely serving children will remain an illusion. Children don't feel secure or have an opportunity to develop and grow until they become part of a loving and permanent "family[27]."

Some will object that, "We don't have the power to do that. There are laws and policies that don't allow it." Where that's true, the solution is simple: Change the policies and laws.

Politics is the art of the possible. In the United States our forefathers bequeathed us a Constitution that grants citizens the power to *"promote the general welfare and secure the blessings of liberty to ourselves and our posterity."* We have the constitutional, spiritual and moral authority to adopt laws necessary to create permanent attachment for children. We've simply lacked the courage, willingness and vision to admit that our current child-welfare system is flawed, broken and must be changed.

For more than two decades, I've been involved in personal and community substance-abuse recovery efforts. I've learned that it is almost impossible to help addicts or alcoholics with depression, employment, relationships, housing, raising children or becoming self-sufficient unless they quit using alcohol and other drugs.

There is a corollary for abandoned, abused and neglected children. We can't help children with poor performance in school, hyperactive behavior, an inability to make friends, depression or self-harming behavior until we create an opportunity for authentic attachment to a permanent family that loves and is capable of caring for them.

The attachment must come first. It is the foundation that everything else rests on. While love and permanency alone aren't always sufficient to help every child, they are as essential to good outcomes for foster children as food and water are to life.

Our current child-welfare system doesn't have the ability to meaningfully measure love or attachment, but our inability to measure something doesn't mean it isn't essential. Scientists didn't "discover" and learn to measure oxygen until the 1770s. Our society's ignorance of the element of oxygen in the composition of air for the years preceding its discovery didn't make oxygen any less essential for our species' survival.

There is reason to have hope about our ability to improve how we take care of children. Most people consider helping kids to be a high priority. The rewards in financial, emotional and spiritual terms are great for society and the individual. The human and financial resources we need to help children are available—they just aren't allocated effectively. The first step in any change is awareness—raising consciousness.

Now that you know, spread the word! Tell anyone who will listen that the current child-welfare system is broken, that real change must be a co-creative effort, that the current system is incapable of proposing the necessary changes itself, and that we must claim and use our power to create loving, permanent relationships for children. If we focus our efforts on these suggestions and principles, we can create a better child-welfare system for the children living in foster care now and for those who are certain to come in the future.

THE ADOPTION PROCESS

Our destiny is to create more and more consciousness. As far as we can discern, the sole purpose of human existence is to kindle a light in the darkness of mere being. —C.G. Jung

The best advice I was given about adoption was that the only people who don't end up with children are the ones who give up. I believe that advice is true, but the process can be discouraging. It is rife with seemingly impossible roadblocks, often followed by unimaginable opportunities. Adoption can be an emotional roller coaster as intense as living with cancer, and success demands that prospective parents "keep their eye on the prize" of adopting a child.

It was important for me to tell many people that I wanted to adopt. Several of my most promising leads, and ultimately how I met Danny, was through a referral to his birthfather from a friend who knew I wanted to be a parent. The power of my desire to have a child, widely communicated, produced amazing results.

It was helpful for me to stay open about the gender, race, age and background of a prospective child. My only rule was that I wanted a kid who was likely to experience normal growth and development. I didn't feel capable of adopting a child with terminal illness or severe developmental delays. I even bent on that when I learned that Danny might have fetal alcohol spectrum disorder (FASD), a condition that could prevent him from having a "normal" life. Fortunately, it turned out that he didn't have FASD.

After I was introduced to Danny, I realized that I was afraid to commit to being his father. I was willing, however, to take small steps toward becoming a family in hopes it might work out. I was scared to let Danny come live with me if it meant I had to adopt him. Instead, I took the attitude that I hoped we could become a family, but the only way to be sure of that was to spend time with each other, live together on a trial basis and see how it worked out. I was often anxious and pessimistic both about my ability to be a parent and Danny's ability to change.

I frequently told myself there would be no shame if I decided I wasn't able to adopt Danny. The only shame was if I ignored my inspiration to try. It takes great courage and endurance to create a family with any adopted child, especially an older special-needs kid. Today, I can't imagine any boy that I would want as my son more than Danny, but that didn't happen overnight. Our attachment took time, effort, patience, mutual respect and love.

The child-welfare system in Washington State has

social workers who specialize in adoptions. One way to find legally free foster children is to meet with an adoption social worker. While the social workers have some flexibility, generally it's helpful to have a home study completed before meeting a prospective child. The social worker can help with getting a home study, or private agencies can provide that service.

Once a home study is completed and approved, it is usually possible to meet a child. I think in most cases it is best that the social worker not immediately tell the child that the person they are meeting is a prospective adoptive parent. It's far too hard on the kid if it doesn't work out. There are many legally free or soon-to-be legally free dependent children in the United States child-welfare system. The adoption social workers struggle to find good homes, so it shouldn't be difficult to arrange an informal meeting with a promising kid. Most social workers have large caseloads and struggle to reply to phone calls, emails and other requests. While it's often frustrating to work with them, it pays to be polite, persistent and patient.

When I decided I wanted to know Danny better, I told his social worker and CASA that I needed to spend time with him. Typically, the social worker will suggest day visits for activities such as going to the park, hiking or watching movies, followed by a single overnight visit that leads to longer stays. For us, some of this was impractical as we lived 130 miles apart.

Eventually, I had to make a decision: Did I want to proceed with adopting Danny? After deciding yes, I had to get Danny permanently placed with me by obtaining a court order for a pre-adoptive home placement. This took persistence and patience. I found it useful to communicate important dates, commitments and concerns to the social worker via email. Social workers have many calls every day; phone calls get forgotten and usually leave no record.

Because there are scores of regulations and rules about safe environments and what is permitted for foster children, the time that Danny lived with me prior to his adoption had extra challenges. The social worker, not me, was his legal guardian. I had to get a court order to take him out of state to visit my family in California and to go on a family cruise to Alaska. There were restrictions on my home (the state didn't like my hot tub or kitchen knives on the counter), and I was told not to leave Danny with anyone who wasn't approved by the state as "safe", which effectively meant I couldn't leave him with anyone unless they completed a time-consuming background check. The only way to get rid of the state's requirements was to complete the adoption.

Unfortunately, the state tends to focus its efforts on children in crisis. Despite receiving enormous amounts of state and federal tax dollars for each foster child, child-welfare services mismanages the money due to a patchwork of bad law, ill-conceived policy and ineffectual practices. The child-welfare system struggles to support children that are doing well. Most of their energies are focused on kids in crisis. When his social worker realized Danny was thriving in my care, she admitted that she didn't have much incentive to keep our case moving toward adoption. She had too many urgent problems to deal with. Moving our adoption forward demanded persistence, patience and relentless advocacy.

Another hurdle was when the social worker asked what legal disclosure I wanted to receive about Danny. In Washington State, social workers are required to share almost all the information they have about a child prior to adoption. This is known as adoption disclosure. When I asked to see everything, I felt I was branded a trouble-maker. My request was met with shock, skepticism and initial resistance. I was informed that most people don't want to "see all the paperwork" and that there were "too many files." I replied that as Danny's prospective parent, I wanted to know as much about him as possible.

I eventually received several thousand pages of documents. Later I discovered that some of the files I should have received were missing—I believe it was more from disorganization than any attempt to conceal information from me.

The files were useful to understand some of Danny's challenges. Though I was aware that much of what I read was from the perspective of a social worker or a visit supervisor, I learned things about Danny that I wouldn't have discovered elsewhere. Reading them helped me become a better parent.

Having my own attorney was crucial to completing the adoption quickly. Although the state offered to help me, several reliable sources told me that the adoption would take much longer if I relied on the state rather than on hiring my own lawyer. Because I hired my own attorney and was persistent, our adoption was completed in just over seven months from the day Danny moved in. It was a relief to be done with the state. Trying to meet their demands was a huge burden. I spent many hours every week dealing with bureaucratic hurdles that added to the stress and challenges in our lives. It's hard enough to try to bond with a special-needs ten-year-old boy without the added burden of the child-welfare system's dysfunctional demands.

The final hurdle was negotiating adoption support. The adoption support worker did her best to misdirect and obfuscate the truth about adoption support subsidies. In 2009 a bill[28] was introduced to the Washington State Senate to require the Department of Social and Health Services to inform prospective adoptive parents about the limits and benefits of receiving adoption support. In the nonpartisan legislative summary of the bill, the point was made that, "The deception that DSHS uses to trick families into adopting children out of the foster-care system should not be allowed."[29]

My experience was that DSHS tried to dishonestly trick me in an effort to save money and move Danny out of their system.

To get the state to offer a reasonable adoption support payment, I had to request a "fair hearing" from an administrative law judge, spend hours researching legal statutes and case law, submit public records requests for two years of emails about adoption support negotiations from every adoption support employee up to and including the Secretary of Department of Social and Health Services (DSHS), request copies of the State and Federal Title IV-E adoption subsidy contract, request copies of the last 20 redacted adoption support agreements cross-referenced with the DSHS foster-child classification, request copies of all adoption support policies not written in DSHS policy manuals or state statute, and request copies of all administrative cases and appeals of adoption support for the past three years.

Although I have no formal legal training, I got advice from attorneys and prepared my brief for the fair hearing. I built a progressively logical case quoting state statutes, federal statutes and excerpts from the 1979 Federal Adoption Support Act. I knew my case was solid, but I had doubts. The bureaucrats I negotiated with are full-time adoption support specialists. They told me I was wrong— that my interpretation of the law was flawed—and that I was hurting Danny by not trusting their recommendation and accepting their offer.

I had excellent legal advice, conducted thorough research and was able to successfully negotiate a reasonable adoption support agreement of about $1,000 a month. It was difficult, time consuming and emotionally draining. My research suggests that other states are just as difficult, or even more so, than Washington. My tenacity translated into an additional $66,000 for Danny's financial support. Adoption support has given me the resources to provide

Danny a personal tutor, highly qualified therapists and many other services that wouldn't be possible without that money.

Most people don't have the time, money and advocacy skills to fight the state. As a result, they are deprived of resources essential to a successful adoption. This is a terrible injustice and another example of how the current child-welfare system harms the children it was established to protect.

Adoption was an arduous process. Initially, many family members and close friends told me I was crazy to consider adopting Danny. Someone I love and respect said, "Of all the bad decisions you've made in your life—and you've made some big ones—your choice to adopt Danny is the worst decision you've ever made." I struggled with that advice. I finally realized it was given in the spirit of someone who loved and wanted to protect me, but I couldn't allow anyone's perspective or advice to diminish my heart's certainty about the wisdom of adopting Danny.

Despite the well-meaning advice of family and friends, and the incredible insecurity I felt in my head, my heart constantly assured me that adopting Danny was my destiny. I experienced many "coincidences" and synchronistic events that confirmed my decision to adopt him. These often happened when I was feeling most discouraged.

What finally convinced me to adopt Danny was recognizing that I was exchanging my wants to meet his needs. I sacrificed my desire for personal freedom, abundant money, sleeping in, taking vacations and going out to dinner with friends to be Danny's dad. It is easy to talk about love and how we are each other's brother and sister, but sometimes spiritual growth demands action. Trading cherished wants for authentic needs is always a good bargain.

Three years after adopting Danny, I don't regret my decision. My friends and family now uniformly say that adopting Danny has been good for both of us. I can't imagine having a child by adoption or birth that feels more like my son than Danny does. How he arrived in my life isn't nearly as important as that he did come to me and we became a family.

Feeling like his father didn't happen overnight—it took lots of time together. But now, more than three years later, the depth of my love and affection for him are immeasurable. I would give my life for him. The two things I am most certain of in life are that the world and I are better off without my drinking alcohol or using other drugs, and that I was meant to be Danny's dad. Everything else flows from these two fundamental beliefs.

I thought I was just getting a kid. What I received was a spiritual opportunity laden with growth, suffering, meaning, depth and joy beyond anything I imagined. While I can't advise anyone whether they should adopt any particular child, I can say that adopting Danny was the right decision for me.

The older I get, the more I believe that some decisions must be made from the heart, not the head, and that our emotional and spiritual experiences as individuals aren't so unique as I once thought. All of us are divine creatures of love, light, shadow and pain. My success with Danny is proof that others can successfully adopt older children too.

Finally, a word of caution. There are two reasons I titled this book *One Kid at a Time*. The first is that a friend wrote to me that I was making the world better one kid at a time. The moment I read that sentence, I realized she was right and that "one kid at a time" was a perfect expression for what I was doing with Danny. The other reason is that I have had to accept that I can't help all the children in need. Trying to save them all myself is hubris, perfectionism and guaranteed failure at its worst. Since adopting Danny, I've been asked to adopt other foster children, and I've said no each time.

All of us have the same 24 hours available to us each day, along with the requirements of taking care of ourselves and those we've chosen to support. I can't help all the children in need. As much as my heart wants to help them all, there is a limit to what my physical body and other resources can accomplish. No one can do it all; we have to help our children together. If I am engaged in service to the greater good, I trust that if I do my part that in the words of the Christian mystic Julian Norwich (1342-1416), *"All shall be well, and all shall be well, and all manner of things shall be well."*

NOTES

CHAPTER 1

1. North American Council on Adoptable Children, http://tiny.cc/chzpz

2. "Thrownaways" is a term defined in the Washington State Department of Social & Health Services Children's Administration Practices and Procedures Guide, whose meaning includes a child who "Has been abandoned or deserted," http://tiny.cc/cr12a

CHAPTER 4

3. For information about the CASA (Court Appointed Special Advocate) program: casaforchildren.org

CHAPTER 16

4. Washington State DSHS Children's Administration Practices and Procedures Guide, Section 4254 Parent-Child-Sibling Visiting Policy, Policy (D): "When siblings are placed apart in out-of-home care, a written plan for twice-monthly visits must be developed (unless safety concerns exist). *Twice-monthly contact during parent-child visits meets this requirement. Other forms of contact may be substituted when a visit is not possible," http://tiny.cc/ulr5k, see also "Braam Settlement": http://braamkids.org/43001.html

CHAPTER 20

5. North American Council on Adoptable Children, http://tiny.cc/navvy

CHAPTER 21

6. O'Hanlon, Timothy, and Laws, Rita. *Adoption and Financial Assistance: Tools for Navigating the Bureaucracy.* Bergin & Garvey 1999

7. Washington State Office of Administrative Hearings, http://tiny.cc/rm29o

CHAPTER 23

8. Casey Family Programs: "Foster Care by the Numbers," http://tiny.cc/ffei4

CHAPTER 28

9. Annie E. Casey Foundation, Financial Information. 2011, http://tiny.cc/mnjc8

10. Child Trends Data Snapshot. May 31, 2011, http://tiny.cc/evc66

11. Annie E. Casey Foundation, "Rebuild the Nation's Child Welfare System," January 2009, http://tiny.cc/ld3wn

12. Study "Midwest Evaluation of the Adult Functioning of Former Foster Youth: Outcomes at Ages 23 and 24." Chapin Hall at the University of Chicago. 2010, http://tiny.cc/35sg4

13. MIT News. "Kids Gain More From Family Than Foster Care," http://tiny.cc/5yojz

14. Study "Midwest Evaluation of the Adult Functioning of Former Foster Youth: Outcomes at Ages 21." Chapin Hall at the University of Chicago. 2007,

http://tiny.cc/zd1t4

15. *ibid*

16. *ibid*

17. Senator Denise Ducheny (D-San Diego), chair of the California Senate Budget Committee speaking before the California Senate on AB 845, http://www.youtube.com/watch?v=Pnkp0dmJEAM

18. Report. United States Government Accountability Office, GAO-12-270T, Foster Children: HHS Guidance Could Help States Improve Oversight of Psychotropic Prescriptions. 2011, http://tiny.cc/0u6gz

19. National Center for Health Statistics. NCHS Data Brief, Number 8, September 2008,

http://tiny.cc/ttog5

20. Tufts Clinical and Translational Science Institute. "Multi-State Study on Psychotropic Medication Oversight in Foster Care." September 2010, http://tiny.cc/ahw02

21. Report. United States Government Accountability Office, GAO-12-270T, Foster Children: HHS Guidance Could Help States Improve Oversight of Psychotropic Prescriptions. 2011, http://tiny.cc/0u6gz

22. Legislative Evaluation & Accountability Program Committee, Washington State Legislature,

http://tiny.cc/85im9

23. Washington State DSHS Children's Administration Practices and Procedures Guide, Section 43105. Extended Foster Care Program, (M). Request court dismissal of the dependency when the youth: (6) Fails to comply with the dependency court order, case plan, placement rules or high school/GED program requirements,
http://tiny.cc/ywtkj

24. Article "This Is Dropout Nation: The Foster Care Ghetto and School Reform. 3/2/11, http://tiny.cc/qk4gh

25. Study "Midwest Evaluation of the Adult Functioning of Former Foster Youth: Outcomes at Ages 21." Chapin Hall at the University of Chicago. 2007,
http://tiny.cc/zd1t4

26. Study "Midwest Evaluation of the Adult Functioning of Former Foster Youth: Outcomes at Ages 23 and 24." Chapin Hall at the University of Chicago. 2010,
http://tiny.cc/35sg4

27. The definition of family as used here includes the concept of tribe, community, nontraditional and nuclear families.

CHAPTER 29

28. Washington State Senate Bill Report, SB5803, "An Act Relating to the Adoption Support Program," as reported by Senate Committee on: Human Services and Corrections, February 20, 2009, http://tiny.cc/serpe

29. *ibid*

BIBLIOGRAPHY

Cline, Foster, and Fay, Jim. *Parenting with Love and Logic (Updated and Expanded Edition)*. NavPress, 2006

Dorris, Michael. *The Broken Cord: A Family's Ongoing Struggle with Fetal Alcohol Syndrome*. HarperCollins, 1989

Eldridge, Sherrie. *Twenty Things Adopted Kids Wish Their Adoptive Parents Knew*. Delta, 1999

Gray, Deborah. *Attaching in Adoption: Practical Tools for Today's Parents*. Perspectives Press, 2002

Keck, Gregory, and Kupecky, Regina. *Adopting the Hurt Child: Hope for Families with Special-Needs Kids*. NavPress Revised, 2009

Keck, Gregory, and Kupecky, Regina. *Parenting the Hurt Child: Helping Adoptive Families Heal and Grow*. NavPress, Revised 2009

O'Hanlon, Timothy. *Practical Guide to Adoption Subsidy for Adoptive Families and Advocates*. Ebook, 2007. Website: http://www.fpsol.com/adoption/guidebook.html

O'Hanlon, Timothy, and Laws, Rita. *Adoption and Financial Assistance: Tools for Navigating the Bureaucracy*. Bergin & Garvey 1999

Savage, Dan. *The Kid: What Happened After My Boyfriend and I Decided to Go Get Pregnant*. Plume, 2000

Streissguth, Ann, and Kanter, Jonathan. *The Challenge of Fetal Alcohol Syndrome: Overcoming Secondary Disabilities*. University of Washington Press, 1997

RESOURCES

ADOPTION
Adopt US Kids: adoptuskids.org
National Adoption Center: adopt.org

ADOPTION SUPPORT
Adoption Subsidy Advocates:
www.fpsol.com/adoption/advocates.html
North American Council on Adoptable Children:
http://tiny.cc/ov8bd

ADVOCACY
Annie E. Casey Foundation: aecf.org
Casey Family Services: caseyfamilyservices.org
Center for Children and Youth Justice: ccyj.org
Child Welfare Information Gateway: childwelfare.gov
Children's Action Network: childrensactionnetwork.org
Congressional Coalition on Adoption Institute:
ccainstitute.org
Dave Thomas Foundation for Adoption:
davethomasfoundation.org
Evan B. Donaldson Adoption Institute: adoptioninstitute.org
Jim Casey Youth Opportunities Initiative:
jimcaseyyouth.org
National CASA (Court Appointed Special Advocates):
casaforchildren.org

Advocacy (continued)
National Foster Parent Association: nfpainc.org
North American Council on Adoptable Children: nacac.org
The Alliance for Children's Rights: kids-alliance.org
Treehouse Foundation: treehousecommunities.org

Fetal Alcohol Spectrum Disorder
FASLink: www.acbr.com/fas/faslink.htm
University of Washington FAS Diagnostic and Prevention
Network: http://depts.washington.edu/fasdpn/

Foster Youth Support
Born This Way Foundation: bornthiswayfoundation.org
Camp to Belong: camptobelong.org
Foster Club: fosterclub.com
The Mockingbird Society: mockingbirdsociety.org
Under One Sky: under1sky.org

Gay Adoption
Families Like Ours: familieslikeours.org
Gay Family Values (extensive state-by-state resource list):
www.gay-family-values.com/gayadoptionresources.html
Gay Parent Magazine: gayparentmag.com

Miscellaneous
Generations Together: generations-together.org

*To receive an updated list of adoption and foster care resources,
or to offer suggestions, please email your request to:
resources@jakedekker.com*

ACKNOWLEDGMENTS

The list of friends and family that made this story possible is another book in itself.

When I told my dad that I intended to write the story of adopting Danny, he said, "Why don't you start your book with Danny's history and all the terrible trials he experienced. Then write about your childhood, and your pathetic life when you were a teenager and young adult, and how you finally overcame your addictions and troubles so you were prepared to become a father. After that, start telling the story of how you met Danny, your experiences trying to work with the state, and all the joys and challenges you had as you tried to become a family." My dad's suggestion gave me the structure for *One Kid at a Time*. As always, my father was a wise guide and mentor to me.

I couldn't have become a parent without the example and love of my mom. She helped with Danny, advised me, and encouraged me to become a good parent every step of this journey. My gratitude for my mom and dad's influence in my life is boundless.

I am indebted to Sukey for copy editing this book and encouraging me to tell this story. Any credit for correct grammar and accuracy belongs to her. The errors remaining are mine. Thank you to Linda for editorial assistance and a lifetime of timely inspiration, and to Claire for the generous contribution of her art. Special thanks to my first draft readers who offered their brilliant suggestions.

The guidance and advice from each of my siblings and their spouses, and my relationships with Jerry, Melinda and Eric were invaluable.

Thank you to Kevin, Donna, Tyrel, Frank, Melissa and Kim for making Danny and me part of your family.

Danny wouldn't be in my life without Franney, Julio and his birth dad. I will always be grateful to each of you for helping Danny and me find each other.

Many friends offered me encouragement and advice through conversations, phone calls and emails during the adoption journey. Your encouragement was the source of great strength, especially during those times when I doubted my ability to become Danny's dad. Thank you to each of you. You know who you are.

Finally, I believe in guardian angels, divine entities and that a loving power greater than ourselves wants to guide us in wisdom, beauty and love. To those ineffable forces I give gratitude, allegiance and love.

Thanks for reading.

Jake Dekker
April, 2012

ABOUT THE AUTHOR

Jake Dekker spent more than two years representing children as a Court Appointed Special Advocate (CASA). He regularly advocates for child welfare and foster care reform. He is working on his next book about children in the child welfare system. If you want to stay informed about how you can help foster kids, please consider any or of the following:

"Like" Jake's author page on Facebook at:
www.fb.com/jakedekkerbooks
Follow Jake on Twitter at: *@jakedekkerbooks*
Send an email to get on Jake's mailing list to:
info@jakedekker.com

For more information on child advocacy and Jake's book, please visit his website:
jakedekker.com

To the Reader

Thank you for reading *One Kid at a Time*. It's a myth that older children aren't adoptable. Tens of thousands of children in the United States are trapped in foster care desperately wishing for a parent. If you would like to share this story, please recommend this book to your friends and family.

Another excellent way to help readers discover this book is for you to write a short, personal review on Amazon.com, BN.com (Barnes & Noble) and Goodreads. com. The only way to get reviews from readers is for you to create them. If reading *One Kid at a Time* was meaningful to you, please consider sharing your experience with others.

I deeply appreciate your helping me share this inspiring story. Together we can create a better future for abandoned, neglected and abused children.

The link to post a review on Amazon is:
amzn.com/1937777014

The link to post a review on Barnes & Noble is:
bn.com (search for *One Kid at a Time*)

The link to post a review on Goodreads is:
goodreads.com (search for *One Kid at a Time*)